COMPREHENSIVE READING STRATEGIES
FOR ALL SECONDARY STUDENTS

COMPREHENSIVE
READING STRATEGIES
FOR ALL SECONDARY STUDENTS

By

DONALD C. CUSHENBERY, ED.D.

Professor of Education
University of Nebraska at Omaha
Omaha, Nebraska

CHARLES C THOMAS • PUBLISHER
Springfield • Illinois • U.S.A.

Published and Distributed Throughout the World by
CHARLES C THOMAS • PUBLISHER
2600 South First Street
Springfield, Illinois 62794-9265

© *1988 by* CHARLES C THOMAS • PUBLISHER
ISBN 0-398-05533-5
Library of Congress Catalog Card Number: 88-24885

Printed in the United States of America
SC-R-3

Library of Congress Cataloging in Publication Data

Cushenbery, Donald C.
        Comprehensive reading strategies for all secondary students
/ by Donald C. Cushenbery.
        p.   cm.
        Bibliography: p.
        Includes index.
        ISBN 0-398-05533-5
        1. Reading (Secondary education) 2. Reading—Remedial
teaching. I. Title.
LB1632.C85   1989
428.4'07'12—dc19
                                                88-24885
                                                CIP

*To all of the students I have been privileged
to teach during the past forty-three years*

PREFACE

The importance of building a high level of competency in all of the major elements of reading has been a major source of emphasis on the part of teachers and parents of elementary pupils for many decades; however, the promotion of a well-designed reading curriculum at the middle, junior, and senior high levels is a fairly recent phenomenon.

Most educational authorities view the area of reading as being a body of skills such as word-attack, comprehension, vocabulary, and study skills that are emphasized in every subject area by each teacher from grades 1–12 who uses print media of any kind. Reading must always be considered a body of skills to be taught by every secondary teacher. In any circumstance, it is not the sole province or responsibility of the English teacher or special remedial reading teacher. Additionally, reading must be individualized as much as possible to insure that all students receive a comprehensive skills program to help each learner attain maximum reading growth. This volume has been constructed as an authoritative source of ready-to-use information for teachers in all secondary subject areas. Special effort has been made to provide data and information relating to twenty reading programs that have been evaluated as being especially innovative and practical.

Chapter I provides a definition of the reading process along with the characteristics of a useful secondary reading program. The importance of various causes of reading difficulty is emphasized in Chapter II. Chapters III, IV and V are devoted to the practical methods for teaching word-attack, vocabulary, comprehension, and study skills. Developing and promoting reading interests is the focus in Chapter VI. Descriptions of twenty exemplary secondary reading programs are included in Chapter VII.

The various subjects discussed in this volume emerged from the results of a study that was conducted with a wide sampling of successful secondary teachers who have a commitment to reading instruction in their respective content areas. The information and suggestions included in each chapter are those that have been proven to be most helpful and practical for teachers with widely varying levels of classroom experience.

D.C.C.

ACKNOWLEDGMENTS

The author wishes to acknowledge his indebtedness to numerous persons who have been of tremendous assistance in the preparation of the manuscript. Appreciation is extended to Mrs. Jean Rutledge for her considerable help in proofreading all of the chapters. Mrs. Becky Schnabel acted as the official courier for the author and a "thank you" is accorded to her.

Sincere appreciation is extended to Mrs. Jan Wiebe, the manuscript typist, for her efficient and dedicated work on this, her fourth volume for the author. Her suggestions for certain changes in the various chapters helped in the development of the total body of material. The permission of Mr. Duane Webb of Sopris West, Incorporated, of Longmont, Colorado to permit the inclusion of several reading programs listed in Edition 13 of the *Educational Programs That Work* is gratefully acknowledged.

Special thanks are to be given to the officials of the twenty schools whose reading programs are discussed in Chapter VII. The names of these persons are included with the descriptive material related to their respective programs. They gave permission to the author to edit their program descriptions to meet space demands. Additional acknowledgment of appreciation is given to many unknown professionals who helped prepare the materials that were sent to the author. The teachers involved in the programs are to be applauded for helping to make the reading curricula effective and exemplary. Lastly, special appreciation is extended to Doctor Virginia Bryg, Omaha Public Schools, who served as special proofreader.

CONTENTS

COMPREHENSIVE READING STRATEGIES
FOR ALL SECONDARY STUDENTS

Chapter I

DEVELOPING AN EFFECTIVE SECONDARY
READING PROGRAM

The area of reading skill development has always held a high priority in the minds of most educators and members of the lay public. According to several national surveys regarding the public's view toward schools, the responsibility of teachers and administrators for helping *all* pupils become functionally literate has always received much attention. While traditionally it has been a universal attitude of both parents and teachers to stress reading instruction at the elementary school level, only recently has a body of thinking developed that notes that reading is a group of recognizable skills which must be continually developed throughout one's lifetime. As a part of this trend, most educators and researchers now believe that an effective, definable program of reading skills development must be established in every secondary school.

This volume has been uniquely designed to be of immediate and practical use for all secondary teachers in planning meaningful lessons which involve the direct teaching of such core components as vocabulary, word-attack, comprehension, study and test-taking skills. Grasping a complete understanding of the place of reading in the total curriculum is basic if secondary teachers are to teach reading skills in the proper amounts at the most teachable moments. In order to provide a meaningful background of understanding with regard to the overall secondary reading program, the following topics are discussed in Chapter I. They are: definition and nature of the reading process; place of reading in the language arts; characteristics of a useful secondary reading program; role of the secondary content teacher in reading instruction; and a summary of the chapter.

DEFINITION AND NATURE OF THE READING PROCESS

The definition of "reading" and the description of the reading process varies with different psychologists, educators, and learning specialists. If you were to ask 100 people to define "reading," you would probably receive 100 different responses. Volumes of books have been written on the subject, frequently with contradictory definitions, each emphasizing a different aspect of the reading process.[1] For some people, proficient reading consists of being able to pronounce orally long lists of words and phrases. Others place much more emphasis on the reading process as the avenue by which one gathers knowledge by having a direct contact with the thoughts and opinions of writers both past and present. A third group of persons views reading as a process by which one can be entertained and amused.

Leading authorities who propose a definitive and precise definition of reading involve a number of common elements in their definitions such as word attack, background of experience, nature and breadth of schemata, and the ability to react to and synthesize large bodies of information and data which are encountered. All of these aspects involve an acceptable level of communication that should and must take place between the writer and the reader. In order to accomplish this goal, the reader must obviously be able to observe various letters and words and react to the auditory cues that bombard his or her environment. Additionally, attention must be given to the mental facets of the reading process such as making comparisons, reacting to controversial concepts, and absorbing those affective elements which will result in the feeling that reading should take place for a number of reasons: learning new cognitive skills; appreciating different kinds of literature; and viewing reading as a generally pleasurable activity.

Throughout the past several decades, numerous models of reading have been devised to attempt to demonstrate to parents, educators, and the general public that the process of reading takes several forms. Briefly stated, those who believe that reading is a *"top-down"* process are of the opinion that adequate comprehension comes about because the learner brings a vast amount of information based on past experiences to the printed page.[2] Those who promote the *"bottom-up"* theory are of the belief that meaning comes from a text-based approach, whereby the majority of meaning comes from the text itself and one's general schemata or background of understanding has a minor role in overall meaning.

Many reading authorities and researchers are of the opinion that the reading process involves both the depth and magnitude of the reader's schemata as well as cues reserved from reading the text material. In most cases the reader aspires to receive the total body of facts and information which the writer wishes to direct to the reader. The degree to which communication takes place is highly dependent upon a number of processes that must be fully operational when the act of reading is taking place.

Visual and Auditory Processes

As noted by Spache and Spache,[3] reading is, first of all, a visual act and it cannot ever be taught soundly if the functions of the eyes are not understood. The reading process begins with a visual impression during which time the eyes focus on the page of print. If effective communication is to be established, it is imperative for both **visual acuity** (the clarity or sharpness of images) and **visual discrimination** (differences in sizes and shapes of letters and words) to be at a highly proficient level.

At a very young age a child's eyes tend to be farsighted, with normal vision being attained at about the first grade level. There are numerous conditions such as astigmatism, nearsightedness, and farsightedness which may afflict the young person when he or she reaches the secondary school level. Some of these conditions can be alleviated or improved through the use of eyeglasses and/or contact lenses which have been prescribed by an **optometrist** or **ophthalmologist**.

By the time many learners reach the secondary level of instruction, they have often developed undesirable visual habits which inhibit such skills as reading comprehension and speed of reading. One of these problems, *regressions*, is the practice of rereading words and/or phrases because inadequate visual contact has been made with the word(s) at the outset. As noted in various locations in this volume, there are numerous strategies that may be undertaken by a secondary teacher to help students overcome regression problems. Those who have very pronounced deficiencies may require the services of a reading specialist or a medical professional who provides eye training programs and exercises.

The role of auditory processes and the ability to develop and maintain a high level of reading skill development must be carefully understood and considered. The origin of many listening difficulties of adolescents can be traced to organic, psychological, and environmental causes. Since much of what is learned by older students and adults is accomplished through the auditory mode, any deficiency in this area should be carefully inspected and remediated as much as possible.

Sequential Abilities

Hopefully, most older students have developed the basic sequential structure of reading by moving from the left to the right side of the page, understanding the syntactical nature of a sentence (subject, predicate, object, modifiers), and noting the logical and reasonable patterns of oral language as they are printed in a book and/or article. The process of reading requires these skills to be in place if the secondary student is to be a proficient reader. There are numerous instructional techniques and materials suggested in this volume for those learners who have limitations in this important area.

Background of Experience Aspect

Since the end product of reading is comprehension or communication, it is necessary for the reader to pronounce or unlock the word and then be able to derive meaning from the word or phrase just analyzed. To accomplish this phase requires that the reader draw on his or her background of experiences which relate to the material just read. Those students who have had extensive training with various types of vocabulary and direct as well as vicarious experiences in the environment are able to develop a more complete level of understanding than those with more meager experiences.

At the secondary level, there are numerous opportunities for supplying experiential concepts to enhance word or phrase meaning. For example, the older student who has performed certain experiments in the physics laboratory should gain the understanding that a **fulcrum** is a type of support on which a lever is placed when a person is trying to move an object. When the physics teacher says this word aloud during the course of a lecture, the learner will immediately reflect on the object he or she has noted earlier. Naturally, one need not insist or require the use of material objects to provide a background of experience, since various other means may be employed to help the reader remember facts and concepts. These may include the use of pictures, bulletin boards, films, computer software programs, and the inclusion of a large amount of supplementary reading in assorted books and publications. For the broadest kind of learning to take place, these indirect activities should be undertaken in **both** the home and school environments. Those secondary students who have had the advantage of taking tours and trips with their parents will generally have a much broader background of experience than less advantaged learners.

Obviously, the nature and kind of background of experience possessed by each learner will differ considerably, and thus the amount of direct teaching of various vocabulary concepts will vary considerably. If several words are to be introduced and taught, the use of a pretest to determine individual and collective knowledge of the pronunciation and meanings of the words should be undertaken. The results should lend a considerable amount of helpful information to the teacher regarding the identification of those students who need additional practice in building a sufficient background of experience or understanding for particular words.

Motivation and Learning

One of the most important processes involved in the act of reading is the level and nature of each learner's level of motivation to want to succeed in performing various reading tasks. Instructors of older students can develop a learning environment that permits a feeling of enjoyment and success to permeate the entire classroom during which time students of all levels of reading ability can benefit. A reward system which recognizes the successes of students needs to be installed whereby learners can benefit from both tangible and intangible awards. The curriculum needs to be structured to such a degree that all students can realize achievement regardless of their background or academic endeavors.

Teachers understand that the physical aspects of the classroom can have a direct bearing with regard to the motivational and learning levels of their students. To help assure that these levels are maximized, careful attention should be given to such items as room temperature, kinds of chairs and tables available, and the amount and kinds of teaching materials used.

To be an effective reader at the secondary level demands a high level of motivation with relevant practice and reinforcement of skills that provide continuous skill development in such important areas as word-attack, vocabulary, and study skills. Each skill must be developed in both subskill and holistic contexts if a high level of reading competency is achieved. A specific individualized program of instruction which is undertaken by all content teachers will help the learner to make meaningful association with various bodies of knowledge. The desire to learn an ever-increasing segment of cognitive and affective skills is highly dependent upon overall motivation to read on the part of the student. The constant practice and reinforcement of words encountered by older learners help them to establish meaningful relationships and associations between printed words and words heard orally and thus is a positive element in vocabulary enlargement.

Affective Aspects and the Reading Process

The relationship between a reader's interest and attitudes with respect to engaging in reading activities has been well established. Those learners who have developed positive attitudes about reading will be much more interested in various reading assignments than those who have a poor self-concept and tend to be negative about such matters. Building an appropriate self-concept is a necessary foundation for effective reading. The experiences required for formulating a healthy desire to read are nurtured first in the home through appropriate modeling of good reading practices and attitudes on the part of family members, especially the parents. As the child enters school, the program of building affective skills must be continued by classroom teachers who demonstrate their love and appreciation for reading.

As learners approach the secondary level, there are many methods or procedures that content teachers can utilize to help each student build numerous affective aspects such as improved self-concept, appreciation for reading in general and books in particular, and positive attitudes with regard to reading and learning. (Further information on such topics as motivational techniques and building lifelong reading interests can be found in Chapter VI.)

First, formulate assignments and activities for individuals and groups of students that are commensurate with their interest and ability levels. To develop a true appreciation for reading demands that success and satisfactory performance be realized. An award system must be in place that will guarantee a measure of positive recognition for the student. Appropriate grading to recognize progression of achievement may be used along with a program of positive written and oral remarks. Some schools have established various types of honor rolls for noting student achievements.

All material assigned for reading should be at the **instructional** reading level. This is the level where the student can demonstrate a silent reading comprehension score of 75–89 percent and an oral reading proficiency of from 95–97 percent. In too many cases, self-concept is damaged because the pupil is required to attempt to read and study from printed material which is at the frustration level. In every instance, the **purpose** for reading should be established in order that a maximum level of comprehension may be realized.

Second, teachers should manage the classroom environment to maximize the opportunities for allowing each student to feel accepted, needed, and wanted. The perceived feelings of the learner with respect to instructor acceptance of his or her academic performance has a direct relationship to the degree of positive self-concept that may be established. There are numerous strategies that may be employed to achieve this goal. These procedures include the discovery of each learner's interest and constructing assignments that correlate with these data. Each person's contributions, however limited, should be recognized. Reading assignments can be taken from a wide and diverse range of materials such as textbooks, resource volumes, and various journals.

Third, relate a student's progress in reading assignments to his or her previous level of achievement. Individual records may be kept by recording progress on separate record sheets or storing on computer software to allow printout sheets which can be easily removed and explained to the learner. In any case, teachers should avoid direct or indirect comparison of student scores. Honest praise of both a verbal and written nature should be incorporated as it seems appropriate.

Associational Aspects and Reading

One of the most significant objectives of any secondary program of reading instruction is that of the enlargement and refinement of the speaking, writing, reading, and potential vocabularies. In order to accomplish this goal, a system of meaning association must be established between the phonemic or spoken elements of words and their graphemic or written counterparts. Unfortunately, many older readers have experienced varying levels of environmental deprivation and thus develop an inherent weakness or limitation for making associations which engender understanding and positive learning situations. Other factors contributing to this type of problem may include excessive school absences due to illness and other reasons, parental rejection and/or apathy, and general lack of motivation on the part of the learner.

An adolescent who seeks to be a proficient reader needs to be provided experiences by classroom teachers which will serve to build relationships and strengthen vocabulary. When providing instruction in vocabulary development, teachers should keep several principles in mind such as: (a) concentration on those words and phrases that the students will encounter in their content assignments; (b) systematic selection of words which are taught in depth; (c) provision for definitional and contextual knowledge of words introduced; and (d) instruction that provides learning the instructional relation to other words previously encountered.[4] (Additional suggestions for building vocabulary and word-associational skills may be found in Chapter III.)

PLACE OF READING IN THE LANGUAGE ARTS

The total area of the language arts in a viable school curriculum consists of the two **expressive** phases of **speaking** and **writing** and the two **receptive** aspects of **listening** and **reading**. Virtually all of the learning of facts, concepts, and attitudes in all of the content areas is obtained through these four avenues. The amount and kind of academic success realized by any one person relates to a significant degree on how well the individual can read, spell, listen, and write. With this in mind, it is important for each content teacher to devise and integrate a well-constructed program of language arts (especially reading) in his or her subject area. Unlike other subject areas, language arts does not have an inherent content. It provides the means to encode language, to translate thought into speech and writing and to decode, to transfer language into meaning and thought.[5]

Many educators and lay persons perceive that reading is at the center of the entire language arts process. For the secondary student to be effective in comprehending print material, each instructor must include a well-planned program of systematic skill strands instruction to help insure that each learner obtains a maximum level of development in the important areas of word-attack, comprehension, vocabulary, and study skills. An approach which encompasses both diagnostic and correct procedures can be installed to assess achievement levels in such important areas as vocabulary and comprehension.

The teaching of reading has a unique relationship to and with language,

since reading instruction involves the student in knowing the relationship between letter-sound relationships and the meaning or message that
those letters and words are supposed to convey.[6] Thus, efficiency in
reading words and deriving appropriate meaning is highly correlated
with good listening skills.

Adolescents across the country speak a number of dialects, and one
may assume that the apparent discrepancy between oral speech sounds
and the graphemic patterns may present a conflict for the learner. For
example, some students have a habit of leaving off the "g" in many words
such as "parkin" for "parking." Others may say "pak" for "park." Teachers
should not necessarily assume that students whose oral speech varies
from standard English will have problems with comprehending print material. The dialect differences that are mostly a matter of pronunciation
have little serious effect on one's ability to read and write. A learner's oral
vocabulary may constitute a minor clue to his or her reading potential.[7]

The relationship between reading and writing is significant to a rather
positive degree, since, for example, the ability to organize words in a
careful syntactical structure is based on one's understanding of meaning
clues and various sentence patterns which are derived from reading
print material. In writing a short story or non-fictional selection which
contains a main idea, the writer needs to perfect silent reading skills to
note the correlation or relationship of main ideas to details and one
detail to another.

Reading is related to listening, since careful listening can help the
learner create optimum levels of development in learning new words
and their use. This information can be extremely helpful to the student
as he or she attempts to pronounce the words and comprehend their
meanings in a multitude of settings.

CHARACTERISTICS OF A USEFUL
SECONDARY READING PROGRAM

The effectiveness of a useful and practical secondary reading program
can be measured according to the degree in which it correlates with the
items that are discussed in the following section. These aspects should be
evident when reading competencies are thought of as a body of skills
which are introduced and taught by the total content faculty of a given
secondary school.

1. **Each content teacher should understand that he or she has a direct**

responsibility to teach each student at his or her present instructional reading level. Despite the earnest endeavors of primary and middle school teachers, many secondary learners cannot demonstrate grade level reading ability. Content teachers cannot be of demonstrable help to a student by issuing constant blame to elementary teachers, lack of books, deficient home environment, student attitudes, and numerous other reasons. The important principle that must be remembered is that **the student needs immediate and long-term help and he or she is enrolled in the instructor's class for as long as 18 weeks.**

Even without formal training in reading methodology, the secondary teacher can use many of the techniques and strategies noted in the remainder of this volume to build reading skill development. The use of a subjective reading inventory, for example, may be utilized to help determine if the class textbook is suitable for use by individual learners. If he or she can demonstrate a 75 percent score on a silent reading comprehension test and correctly pronounce at least 95 percent of the words aloud, one may decide informally that the text is appropriate for use with that individual. If the learner scores below these standards, the teacher can make immediate plans for providing alternative materials which are written at a lower grade level. Conversely, if a more gifted reader scores considerably in excess of these standards, more challenging materials must be obtained. Additional helpful diagnostic data may be secured through the utilization of informal cloze tests and a careful study of standardized achievement test results.

2. **A well-organized program of reading skills development requires the construction of developmental, remedial, and corrective reading programs.** Each content teacher needs to construct lesson plan strategies to assure that all secondary students develop certain basic, **developmental** reading skill competencies if they are to read and comprehend class texts and related print materials.

A **remedial** program should be established and directed by a reading specialist for those learners who exhibit especially serious reading problems and cannot be served adequately by the classroom content teacher. Remedial reading is intended for students who are reading on levels roughly two or more years below their capacities. These students are taught by instructors familiar with diagnostic procedures for identifying specific weaknesses and appropriate methods for overcoming them.[8]

A **corrective** reading program may be constructed by a content teacher to help correct a common reading deficiency that may be in evidence for an entire class or group. For example, the social studies teacher may find that his or her second-hour world history class may lack skills in adjusting reading rate for studying certain chapters or units in the class text. The instructor may desire to set aside one or more class periods for the expressed purpose of demonstrating and explaining the various reading rates and how each relates to given questions or purposes for reading.

3. **Many different kinds of instructional materials can be assembled by teachers and administrators to help meet the varied needs of the students who may have widely diverse reading levels.** In any class, one may find a wide range of reading ability levels represented. For example, an instructor may use the formula, two-thirds times the mean chronological age of the students in a class, to receive an estimate of the number of reading levels that may be present. In a tenth grade class where one might have a mean chronological age of 15, as many as ten or more reading levels may be in evidence. With this in mind, the secondary teacher may find some of the tenth grade learners reading as low as the fifth grade level and some as high as the university or college level. An analysis of these data leads one to the inescapable conclusion that no **one** textbook or study guide can possibly meet the instructional needs of all students in a particular class.

Instructors who develop a truly individualized reading program based on ability and learner interest will allow each student to choose a book or other kind of print media which relates to his or her reading ability level. In order for this situation to be realized, it is necessary and important to have a wide variety of books readily available. Contrary to the opinion of some teachers and lay persons, many below average readers are not embarrassed to read from less difficult books, because they are able to achieve success and read and remember information required by content teachers.

4. **A well-designed program of reading evaluation should be constructed which employs the use of both formal and informal instruments and techniques.** The major purpose of evaluation is to provide relevant data to instructors for improving the reading instructional programs for learners in both the individual and collective realms. Evaluation is a continuous process that involves a global set of strategies and tools including commercial tests, teacher-made instruments, and structured observation of student reading habits and abilities. All testing tools have inherent strengths and limitations; thus, the secondary content teacher must necessarily utilize testing instruments which are valid for a wide range of purposes.

For example, commercial standardized secondary tests (e.g. *Nelson-*

Denny) yield valuable data with regard to the level of a student's level of reading skill development in such important areas as vocabulary, comprehension, and rate of reading. Other types of information desired such as the current instructional reading level can be obtained through the administration of a subjective reading inventory and/or a cloze procedure. Affective domain aspects such as reading interests and overall attitudes with regard to the reading act can best be judged by listening carefully to the oral comments of students and observing their silent reading strategies and habits. An evaluation of the present reading skills and attitudes can be constructed from a careful investigation of the patterns of scores and data from all types of commercial and informal instruments that are employed.

An important purpose of all evaluative testing is to supply the instructor with reliable information relating to such vital decisions as the type and kinds of instructional materials to use with individual students, how to pace instruction, and the approximate potential learning level of a student. An exhaustive treatise of the total topic of reading evaluation can be found in several of the texts cited in the references at the close of each chapter in this volume as well as a recent volume written by the author (*Improving Reading Skills in the Content Area*, Springfield, IL, Charles C Thomas, 1985).

5. **The philosophy must be established that reading is not a separate and distinct subject but rather a body of distinct skills which should be introduced and taught at all grade and learning levels.** Some educators and parents are of the belief that the basic reading competencies of word attack and comprehension should be attained by the time a student completes the sixth grade. All of these competencies and skills need to be reinforced and strengthened at the junior and senior high levels. A few selected learners may need individualized lessons to strengthen such areas as critical reading, study skills, and reading rate. Certain affective domain segments, such as reading appreciation and detecting mood and feelings of writers, may require attention by content teachers. The skills noted earlier in this chapter should be expected of each learner; thus, individual students should be carefully evaluated through the use of both formal and informal strategies and techniques to determine the rather precise dimensions which should be established for their developmental, remedial, and corrective reading programs.

6. **A program of instruction should be developed to help each secondary student to study and comprehend the information found in textbooks and reference materials that are common to a particular content area.** In the area

of world history, for example, it is important for the instructor to explain the unique features of the text and related books such as various glossaries, summaries, reference sections, and timelines. Science and mathematics instructors may need to provide special presentations in order for students to understand the meanings of various charts and graphs. Because many content books contain a significant body of data in a limited amount of space, necessary instruction must be provided for guiding learners to make important decisions regarding which statements should be remembered in detail for completing class tests and projects. Students need to be able to read with a distinct purpose in mind and at a rate that is commensurate with the kind of facts and principles to be remembered. Accordingly, guidance should be given to students relating to the skills involved in detailed reading, skimming, and scanning.

7. **Appropriate in-service training should be provided for those secondary teachers who need further information regarding instructional procedures and strategies for helping students improve basic reading skills.** Due to the fact that many secondary instructors have not completed formal university and college reading methods courses, there may be a need for well-planned in-service courses and workshops that are directed by the school system or university reading specialist. In some school districts, committees of teachers from the various content areas are formed to undertake the construction of curriculum and/or study guides which may prove helpful for all types of learners as well as experienced and inexperienced teachers. A vital component of such meetings consists of teaching demonstrations by the reading or curriculum specialist to indicate the best methods to employ for building vocabulary, comprehension, study skills, and resource reading strategies. Follow-up activities by the workshop director may include observation of classroom teachers with subsequent conferences which may provide constructive suggestions for improvement of reading skill components during future class sessions. Throughout all of the sessions, each instructor should develop the philosophy that **every teacher is a reading teacher.**

ROLE OF THE SECONDARY CONTENT TEACHER IN READING INSTRUCTION

If an effective reading program is to be developed according to the principles described in the previous section, each teacher in the secondary school will fulfill certain assignments. The suggestions noted in this section can be undertaken by any and all teachers in a satisfactory manner regardless of the subject being taught. A concerted effort by the total faculty will help each learner to realize a level of maximum growth in basic skill areas noted in an earlier section of this chapter.

1. **The instructor must explain the purposes for reading when a given chapter, book, or article is to be studied as a class assignment.** For many years reading researchers have determined through a careful study of data from controlled studies that **lack of purpose for reading** is one of the leading causes of poor comprehension.

In many instances a well-meaning and experienced teacher may realize that the time for a class period has elapsed and that tomorrow's reading assignment must be given immediately. Accordingly, he or she says in a loud voice, "Read the next chapter and we'll discuss it in class tomorrow. Remember to read it carefully, because I may give you a short test over it!" In the American history class the next chapter is entitled "President Wilson and World War I." The chapter contains dozens of facts, figures, and difficult concepts, and most students are unsure of what kinds of information should be remembered. Since the section is 23 pages in length, many average learners may be content to remember a few general concepts and ignore important details. Due to the fact that the teacher and learner may have very different ideas about what is to be comprehended, the student may possibly attempt to remember long lists of facts and figures that the instructor feels are unimportant and thus are not required on an examination.

To give appropriate and reasonable purposes for reading, a list of guiding questions can be constructed that involve common goals of teachers and learners. These questions should be stated carefully and thoroughly understood by all readers **before** they begin a specified silent-reading assignment.

2. **Secondary content instructors should encourage their students to develop competency at all three levels of comprehension.** A casual observation and inspection of the types of written and oral questions constructed by some teachers appear to indicate that much importance is placed on a learner's ability to read and remember a significant number of details and facts obtained from their silent reading assignments. As noted in Chapter IV of this volume, there should be direct attention given to **all** three levels of comprehension: literal, interpretive, reading, and critical. Many situations will arise in the life of every person that will demand "reading

between the lines" and/or making a decision whether a given statement is a fact or an opinion.

Readers are forced to deal with critical and creative issues and project his or her feelings with regard to the material being read. Contrasts are imperative between what the student knows about a subject and how a writer actually treats the topic. Showing students how to make critical judgments of print media in terms of established facts will help them to read and comprehend with the highest level of proficiency.

3. **One of the important goals of any secondary content instructor should be that of improving a learner's personality through a meaningful reading skills curriculum.** There are numerous objectives and goals that should be pursued in developing cognitive, affective, and psychomotor skills in reading. Merely reading a single textbook in order to remember a myriad of facts and figures demanded by the teacher does little to introduce students to dozens of volumes which may cause them to laugh, cry, or stimulate their thinking in other ways. They are generally interested in reading affective material if they are introduced to it appropriately. The modeling of the teacher is important, since he or she must demonstrate that he or she reads widely for a multitude of purposes.

The use of books for bibliotherapy can be very useful, especially in literature classes. Many studies have pointed out that peer influence is a significant factor with regard to choice of books to be read. "Advertising" books to all students can be undertaken by all teachers. Reading **must** be presented as an enjoyable activity which can result in the accumulation of new facts, concepts, and attitudes.

SUMMARY

The nature of the reading process involves a number of significant factors including those in the areas of physical, emotional, and mental functions. Reading is one of the most important of all of the language arts and should be promoted as a body of skills to be taught and reinforced by all teachers. The successful secondary reading program is characterized by many important facets that are described in this chapter. Each teacher has an important role to fulfill such as asking appropriate questions, establishing purposes for reading, and improving self-image through the use of interesting supplementary print materials.

REFERENCES

1. Lapp, Diane and James Flood. *Teaching Students to Read.* New York, Macmillan, 1986, p. 5.
2. Heilman, Arthur W., Timothy R. Blair, and William H. Rupley. *Principles and Practices of Teaching Reading* (Sixth Edition). Columbus, Charles E. Merrill, 1986, p. 4.
3. Spache, George D. and Evelyn B. Spache. *Reading in the Elementary School* (Fifth Edition). Boston, Allyn and Bacon, 1986, p. 7.
4. Vacca, Jo Anne L., Richard T. Vacca, and Mary K. Gove. *Reading and Learning To Read.* Boston, Little, Brown, 1987, pp. 183–185.
5. Coody, Betty and David Nelson. *Teaching Elementary Language Arts.* Belmont, California, Wadsworth Publishing Company, 1982, p. 2.
6. Heilman, Arthur W., Timothy R. Blair, and William H. Rupley. *Principles and Practices of Teaching Reading* (Sixth Edition). Columbus, Charles E. Merrill, 1986, p. 29.
7. Early, Margaret and Diane J. Sawyer. *Reading To Learn in Grades 5 to 12.* New York, Harcourt Brace Jovanovich, 1984, p. 22.
8. Karlin, Robert. *Teaching Reading in High School* (Fourth Edition). New York, Harper and Row, 1984, p. 17.

Chapter II

UNDERSTANDING THE CAUSES OF READING DIFFICULTIES IN THE SECONDARY SCHOOL

There is considerable evidence from various local and national studies of reading achievement to suggest that the vast majority of secondary students can read satisfactorily for their grade and learning levels. Unfortunately, 10 to 20 percent of a typical school population must be considered retarded or disabled readers due to a significant number of factors or conditions that appear to inhibit their abilities to read grade level print media.

The problem reader reads typically below grade level and probably exhibits several traits such as poor self-concept, improper personal adjustment, and general inability to pronounce and comprehend simple words and phrases. Accordingly, he or she may find it necessary to develop various psychological mechanisms such as avoidance, compensation, and aggressive or shy behavior to cope with everyday reading assignments. These learners should be exposed to a program of planned remedial instruction that will help improve both basic reading skills and overall personality development. The teaching environment must be structured to allow a maximum level of reading improvement to be realized, since "nothing breeds success like success."

The causes of ineffective reading are numerous and varied, and each has a varying level of importance with respect to the overall pattern of reading difficulties displayed by any one learner. The point is that you need not be unduly concerned with which cause or area of causation may be responsible for the reading failure. What teachers need to know is how a specific person deals with language, learning, the reading processes, and the world in which he lives as a human being.[1]

Some writers in popular journals and books have a tendency to promote the myth that **the** cause of reading failure of adolescents is either: (a) the learner has not been taught a sufficient amount of phonics; or (b) elementary reading instruction has been deficient. Further, some of the writers proceed to describe a particular reading approach (usually phonics-based) that represents a "new breakthrough" in reading. Most current reading researchers hold the point of view that reading retardation is generally the result of a combination of several important factors such as neurological impairments, learning disabilities, deficient socioeconomic environment, faulty educational experiences, frequent change of schools, emotional problems, physical handicaps, and a poor background of experience.

To evaluate the precise causal factors requires the careful selection and administration of commercial and informal testing instruments and strategies. Many of the causes will expose themselves as teachers work with secondary students and functionally diagnose his or her problems within the context of a stimulating program of instruction and a warm personal relationship.[2]

If secondary teachers are to help retarded readers, an understanding must be gained relative to the importance of each of the major commonly noted causes of reading failure. In order to accomplish this purpose, the following topics are discussed in this chapter: emotional conditions and reading ability; socioeconomic factors; physical aspects and reading; educational experiences and reading success; role of neurological factors; and the influence of intellectual levels and reading ability.

EMOTIONAL CONDITIONS AND READING ABILITY

A casual observation of the completed case studies of numerous adolescents who are severely retarded in reading leads one to conclude that there is a significant relationship between emotional problems and reading failure. The teenager who exhibits a high level of difficulty with the reading act frequently develops obvious emotional tendencies such as aggressive behavior, withdrawal, and shyness.

When careful studies are made of the causes and conditions surrounding the problems of disabled readers, an emotional difficulty is often found to be present. Even when an emotional problem has been identified and seems to have a causal relationship to the reading difficulty, one must remember that other students with similar emotional problems read well. Often, it is the combination of an emotional problem with a visual defect or other difficulty such as absence at crucial times for learning that centers the focus of the problem on reading.[3]

The emotional difficulties of an adolescent reader have no doubt developed over a long period of time. Dechant[4] suggests aspects such as the following may create emotional problems: difficulties in adjusting to a new environment; poor parent-child relationships; sibling rivalry; lack of encouragement from home; and negative attitudes of parents to learning in general. Students may feel that they are "no good" and thus are sure that they cannot succeed in reading tasks.

Serious concept problems of older readers may develop through no direct fault of their own. They feel humiliated because they are labeled as poor readers and placed in special classes. Because of numerous difficulties in the home such as parental rejection or peer disapproval at school, they make the unfortunate conclusion that there is something wrong with them and they can never succeed at any task, especially in those academic assignments that require successful reading and comprehending.

A review of the detailed case studies of numerous adolescents reveals that there is a great likelihood that the student in question has had, or will have, one or more emotional problems. One must remember that emotional problems can create reading difficulties **or** a severe reading deficiency may cause emotional problems. Whatever the case, the learner who has severe emotional problems should be referred to appropriate school and community specialists and psychologists, social workers, and psychiatrists due to the fact that many classroom teachers are without the proper professional training to help the learner cope in the teaching-learning environment. A report should be compiled by the specialist to be shared with the classroom teacher relative to the impact of the emotional difficulties on reading achievement along with recommendations for the appropriate educational program which should be provided for the learner. Integrating the recommendations and suggestions from such a report should help the secondary teacher to plan the type of developmental and/or remedial instructional curriculum that will result in maximum academic success for the affected learner.

SOCIOECONOMIC FACTORS

The student's socioeconomic status has a significant influence on the degree to which he or she succeeds in mastering reading skills. Though there has been a long and continuous debate and discussion relating to the degree of importance of heredity and environment, one must conclude that both are vital if success in reading is to be achieved. Quarreling parents, broken homes, child neglect, child abuse, overprotection, parental domination, anxiety, hostility, or destructive rivalry among siblings are likely to create problems of security and well-being.[5]

Many adolescents come from home environments where the cultural and language background is quite different from that encountered in the school setting. Too many teachers are inadequately prepared to understand or accept cultural values that are different from their own. To teach these students successfully, instructors must be cognizant of these differences and must, above all else, seek to understand and not disparage ideas, values, and practices different from their own.[6]

The present reading difficulties of many adolescents began at a very early age because of certain home conditions. Of all of the activities that can occur in the home prior to a child's first grade entrance, one factor has been found by research to be the most influential on a child's success in beginning reading. Most reading specialists consider it to be **reading to the preschool child.**[7] Additionally, some students have parents who make unfavorable comparisons between and among siblings that can easily create a spirit of hatred and insecurity. This type of environment creates a possible feeling of basic insecurity leading to the belief that "I will never be a good reader!" The effect of the home environment and the parents' attitude toward their children's reading attitude was found to be very important according to a study recently completed by Bates and Navin.[8] They undertook an experimental study group with a group of parents whose children (grades 4 through 9) were enrolled in a university remedial reading tutoring program. An analysis of test data derived from attitude and comprehension tests given to the learners resulted in a very obvious finding that counseling parents of remedial readers does improve the students' reading comprehension and attitudes.

A relatively new sociological trend has developed in the home conditions of many learners. There are hundreds of adolescents who live with family members in makeshift shanties and in various environments which tend to accelerate feelings of insecurity and generally poor adaptation to given school situations. Many of them lack the basic needs of food and clothing.

The absence of interesting reading materials in the home can have a decided negative effect on the degree of reading interest shown by an individual student. The authors of one detailed study[9] analyzed their data and concluded that those students who ranked high in reading and language development also came from homes where a sizable variety of reading materials could be found.

Parental attitudes with regard to the value of reading can have either positive or negative modeling effects on the adolescents in the family. If they have observed for many years that their parents never engage in reading activities, they are likely to gain the impression that interest in and ability to read is not an important priority. Conversely, if parents demonstrate an interest in reading, their children may be prone to develop a high level of interest in reading. Teachers and administrators must remember that they, too, are role models and should, through their daily interactions with adolescents, demonstrate the value of reading and learning.

The authors of the prestigious publication *Becoming A Nation of Readers: The Report of the Commission on Reading*[10] concluded that parents play roles of inestimable importance in laying the foundation for learning to read and that they have an obligation to support their children's continued growth as readers. They need to facilitate the growth of their children's reading by taking them to libraries, encouraging reading as a free-time activity, and supporting homework.

To help alleviate the limiting aspects of a disadvantaged environment, Congress passed the Elementary and Secondary Education Act of 1965 which provided funds under Title I for building enrichment programs in the areas of reading and mathematics. (More recently, this agency has been retitled Chapter I.) To help these learners gain new reading skills, a recent study[11] by the U.S. Office of Technology Assessment concluded that nearly 60 percent of all Chapter I teachers reported the use of computers, and spending for computers amounted to approximately $89,000,000 during the period from 1980 to 1985. According to the report, there is a general belief among researchers and practitioners that computer technology enhances motivation for learning. (The 1988 Budget plan approved by the Senate raises funding by $100,000,000 over the 1987 level and would allow the Chapter I program to serve an additional 700,000 students but still far fewer than the 4.8 million students who are eligible.[12]

PHYSICAL ASPECTS AND READING

As noted in the previous chapter, there are numerous aspects of the physical realm of the learner. Deficiencies in the areas of vision, hearing, and general health can have a serious negative effect on the reading skill growth patterns of adolescents. A brief discussion of each of these aspects is included under this heading.

Vision

Though there is a lack of precise research evidence to establish a positive relationship between individual eye problems and reading disabilities, there appears to be sufficient data to suggest that more retarded than average readers possess various eye disorders. A single vision disorder such as hyperopia or myopia rarely creates reading difficulties; however, when the condition is coupled with various other disabilities, it can have a definite negative impact on a secondary student's ability to read proficiently.

An analysis of several investigations appears to indicate that severe muscular imbalance can result in much visual discomfort and create a condition which may cause an individual to want to avoid reading. To assess these and other problems, the student should be referred to an optometrist or ophthalmologist for a complete medical examination. The school nurse may use various instruments as screening devices such as the *Massachusetts Vision Test, Keystone Visual Survey Test, AO School Vision Screening Test,* and the *Ortho-Rater.*

Vision difficulties need to be alleviated as much as possible before a concerted remedial program is undertaken. These measures include the use of prescription eyeglasses, contact lens, and eye exercises including orthoptic programs that are offered by various optometrists. Teachers may wish to make changes in the classroom setting by allowing the student to sit at the front of the room or providing books and other materials with sight-saving print. He or she may contact one or more community agencies for financial help for those students whose parents cannot afford to purchase eyeglasses or contact lens.

Hearing

Students who have hearing deficits may have a considerable amount of difficulty with reading skill assignments for at least three significant reasons: (a) pupils normally learn to speak through listening; thus vocabulary and sentence pattern formations may be deficient if adequate hearing is not present; (b) learners cannot perceive auditory differences in words; and (c) they cannot gain benefits from class discussions or follow directions given by the teacher.[13] Those students who have severe hearing loss may encounter much difficulty if instructors emphasize a strong phonetic approach to learning. Visual modality methods which utilize charts, maps, and similar objects must be used. Providing written announcements and directions should be made for hearing-impaired students.

Secondary teachers need to be alert for certain manifestations and tendencies that may be exhibited by individual students. These would include head movement, cupping the hand over the ear, and repeated requests to have oral comments repeated. The speech and language specialist (or audiologist) should employ the use of an audiometer to detect the degree of hearing loss for pure tones of low, medium, and high pitches. Any student who demonstrates a hearing loss of 20–25 decibels should be referred to an ear specialist for further evaluation. The content teacher should utilize the contents of the evaluative report to make necessary changes in instructional procedures to better accommodate the reading instructional program for the adolescent. These may include asking the learner to sit at the front of the classroom and speaking at a higher volume when giving directions or announcements.

General Health Factors and Reading

One or more serious health conditions can have a delimiting effect on the progression of reading skill development. The following aspects are some of the more common health problems encountered by secondary students which have an effect on reading improvement.

1. **Muscular Coordination.** While there appears to be inconclusive evidence of a strongly positive relationship between muscular coordination and ability to read, special attention should be given to any learner who has had any type of brain injury or neurological disorders that results in poor muscular coordination with regard to the use of the eyes or arms. Some researchers such as Newell C. Kephart, Pearl Rosborough, and Marianne Frostig contend that the entire area of lateral dominance and muscular coordination has a significant relationship to reading ability and should receive much attention from educators.

2. **Illicit Drugs and Alcohol.** At the present time the use of illicit drugs by adolescents is at an all-time high. Sue Rusche, a national authority on drug abuse from Atlanta, Georgia, estimates that by the time a freshman boy or girl becomes a senior, two-thirds of the kids in her class will have used an illicit drug. One in five will be a problem drinker. Two in five will consume five or more drinks in one sitting. The use of these drugs and alcohol has a disastrous effect on the brain and inhibit vital mental

processes for learning reading mastery concepts and remembering basic facts and main ideas.

Secondary teachers should follow school policy guidelines and take appropriate action, such as making referrals, to help alleviate the problem. Appropriate sessions with school counselors and reading specialists may yield valuable suggestions for classroom teachers in the process of lesson planning for the present and future. Of all of the factors related to deficient reading ability, the facet of illicit drugs and alcohol may be the most urgent and important deterrent to satisfactory reading.

3. Chronic Illness. Prolonged illness such as rheumatic fever, heart trouble, various infections, malnutrition and related problems may influence negatively the reading skills progress of the secondary student. During the period of absence, the individual misses learning important reading skills. If the illness has been of an extended nature, basic deficiencies in the important areas of word-attack, comprehension, and study skills may result.

Additionally, many of these physical problems decrease the learner's overall energy and motivational level, and he or she finds it difficult, if not impossible, to maintain a desire to learn. Teachers with these types of students should solicit help and guidance from school and community counselors in order to plan an adequate program of instruction.

4. Malnutrition. Due to the sizable increase in the number of homeless and unemployed adults in the United States, numerous conditions such as poverty, inadequate housing, and poor diets have evolved including pathetic cases of advanced malnutrition. This condition creates an unsatisfactory setting that makes the learning of basic literacy skills extremely difficult for some adolescents. Students in this category should be made aware of school and community meal programs such as free or reduced-rate breakfasts and lunches.

5. Glandular Difficulties. The endocrine glands in the human body perform vital functions involving such aspects as body growth and weight, energy level, and emotional conditions. Those learners who have glandular malfunctions may show evidence of small size, obesity, mental sluggishness, and nervous tendencies. Many adolescent retarded readers are afflicted with these kinds of problems. For some patients, the administration of certain medical injections and prescription products has had a dramatic and positive impact on the growth of general academic abilities, especially those in the area of reading and the remainder of the language arts. All adolescent students who demonstrate pronounced reading difficulties should be advised to have a comprehensive physical examination to determine the degree of any glandular problems that may be present, if any.

EDUCATIONAL EXPERIENCES AND READING SUCCESS

Many years ago, most of the schools in the United States had a regulation that if a student did not demonstrate adequate grade level performance in the basic skills areas such as reading, he or she would not be allowed to enroll for the next grade. In some elementary schools as many as 15 to 20 percent of the pupils were retained.

In more recent years, a policy of nearly universal promotion has developed because of a number of reasons. **First,** there is research to suggest that, in some cases, retention does not result in the type of growth which may be expected because of pupil resistance to learning and other factors. **Second,** some states and local school districts require parent permission for retention. Many parents refuse to permit their child to be retained and therefore the child progresses to the next learning level with noted deficiencies in some basic reading skill competencies.

From a very careful study of present educational policies that are being followed in some school systems, one must conclude that certain past instructional plans **may** have been a contributing cause of some of the reading skill proficiencies of adolescent students. The following is a list of suggested educational changes for improving adolescent reading skills.

1. **The 1987 data from the National Assessment of Educational Progress study indicate some alarming conditions that presently exist among teachers and schools according to LaPointe.**[14] These include: (a) 40 percent of 13-year-olds could not read their textbooks with ease; (b) for the 9-to-13-year-old groups, no growth in reading achievement took place between 1980 and 1984; and (c) only about 10 percent of the 9-year-olds had recently read a book or novel. While the total data suggest that pupils generally have positive attitudes about reading, they fail to recognize the crucial importance of reading in real life. **In summary, all teachers need to stress reading comprehension skill development and help students build more positive attitudes about the value of reading skills for improving academic functions.**

2. **Pupils should spend less time completing worksheets and skill pages.** Though these activities consume a sizable amount of the classroom

instructional time in American classrooms, there is little evidence that these activities are related to reading achievement. These activities should be reduced to the minimum.[15]

3. There should be more emphasis placed on a global reading readiness program that stresses an interdeveloped reading, writing, and oral language program. Many activities presently undertaken such as coloring, cutting with scissors, and discriminating shapes actually do little to promote reading development.

4. Non-academic activities involving group time teaching, telling of stories to the class, arts and crafts, active play, use of toys and puzzles, and academic games have negative correlations with achievement gain. Similar results also hold true for secondary school students where the frequency of social interactions had consistently negative correlations with student reading achievement gain.[16]

5. Many instructors at both the elementary and secondary levels who have major responsibilities for teaching reading skills have had a limited amount of training for undertaking their assignments. This condition may cause some pupils to lack instruction in some very basic skill components and thus be the catalyst for becoming a deficient reader. Unfortunately, many states still do not **require** secondary teachers to complete a reading methods course and thus they are not generally prepared to cope with the students who exhibit numerous reading difficulties.

An impressive study conducted by Rexel Brown[17] was designed to determine if the number of graduate reading courses completed by a teacher had a relationship with the effectiveness of the teacher when instructing pupils in the areas of vocabulary and comprehension. He found a significant relationship did exist, since the mean pupil gain in vocabulary favored teachers with two or more courses in reading, and, while not reaching significance, the mean gain in comprehension and total reading favored those teachers who had completed course work.

6. In some instances, improper reading instruction is designed for students that may lead students to dislike reading and feel frustrated with reading tasks. For example, some teachers make the assumption that the reading grade placement score obtained from a typical reading achievement test represents the valid instructional reading level of the student. Actually, test scores tend to be much higher than actual achievement levels due to the guessing factor. To find the true level of achievement requires careful observation and the administration of well-developed, nationally recognized individualized reading tests such as the *Spache Diagnostic Reading*

Scales, Durrell Analysis of Reading Difficulty, and the *Gates-McKillop-Horowitz Reading Diagnostic Test.* To achieve the ideal teaching-learning environment requires that a match be made between the difficulty level of the print media being used and the learner's actual instructional level.

7. **Some reading instructional materials used at the elementary school levels have very limited vocabularies and restricted story selections which may actually inhibit a learner's ability to experience reading growth at the secondary level.** Bettelheim and Zelan[18] contend that the simplicity of sentences does not encourage investment of mental energy in reading, nor permit the conveyance of anything interesting. The diction is literally "baby talk" with an endless repetition of identical words that discourages the child and interferes with intellectual development.

8. **The absence of a well-devised individualized reading program at the elementary school levels may be the cause of some reading retardation cases at the secondary level.** There may be some instances when teachers feel reluctant to allow pupils to move at their own rate, because they believe that they should read from grade level basal readers regardless of the pupil's **actual** everyday instructional reading level. If this situation exists over a long period of time, the learner may become very discouraged because he or she "cannot keep up" with the rest of the pupils. The establishment of an individualized reading program is imperative if the student is to make maximum progress and be motivated to learn.

9. **A few elementary schools have a limited scope and sequence of reading skills for the total mastery of basic reading skills, and thus some important skill areas may not receive sufficient attention.** One of the most important skill areas that should get maximum attention is the area of phonics. The value of intensive phonics instruction has been known for some time beginning with the findings of the *First Grade Studies* in the late 1960s. Dykstra[19] found the code emphasis programs consisting of the phonics-first basals and the linguistic readers resulted in better oral word pronunciation and silent word recognition skills than did the conventional meaning-emphasis basal reading programs. As of 1984, Pearson[20] noted that the results of recent comparative studies still suggest that programs emphasizing early, reasonably intensive phonics instruction produce readers who are more proficient at word recognition than programs emphasizing meaning. There is, however, a possibility that heavy emphasis on phonics may negatively affect comprehension ability and perhaps affective aspects of reading as well.

10. **Since every learner has a preferred learning modality (e.g. visual,**

auditory, kinesthetic), it is important for teachers at the pre-secondary levels to alter teaching procedures to allow for these conditions. In an alarming number of cases, teachers may assume that all pupils are auditory learners and thus insist on using the lecture method of instruction. Those students who are visual learners will gain knowledge at an unsatisfactory level. To correct this situation requires the administration of various tests to derive desired modality information. Individualized curriculum provisions for each learner should follow.

THE ROLE OF NEUROLOGICAL FACTORS

The neurological processes involved with reading skill development are both complex and varied. The brain must function in the correct manner if visual images are to be assimilated and comprehension obtained. Teachers and reading specialists must be alert with regard to observing students and noting any obvious symptoms of brain damage, such as inappropriate motor difficulties, and orientation problems, such as the inability to follow visually a line of print or underline words or phrases with a writing instrument.

A careful assessment of a given student's neurological condition should be undertaken as a team effort involving the school psychologist and various medical specialists such as neurologists. They may find that malfunctioning of the brain may have been caused at a much younger age due to one or more of the following conditions: (a) irregular growth pattern of the brain which creates a delayed response to daily reading and learning activities; (b) defects occurring at birth or at a later time resulting in undeveloped areas of the language cells of the brain; (c) damage to the brain caused by encephalitis and related diseases which severely retard normal language function growth; (d) injury to the brain occurring at the time of birth; and (e) brain disease due to chemical imbalances.

The difficulties just cited can be responsible for a variety of learning problems such as **dyslexia** and **hyperactivity**. These two difficulties are found to be quite common among many adolescent students who have pronounced reading difficulties. Because of the magnitude of the importance of these conditions, further brief data are presented regarding the description, diagnosis, and treatment of each aspect.

Dyslexia

A review of the pertinent history of disabling reading conditions reveals that educators and medical specialists have provided varied definitions of the term. As far back as 1917, Doctor James Hinshelwood, a Scottish doctor, contended in his writing that the loss of visual memory centers in the brain could create a reading problem. Later, Doctor Samuel Orton, a famous Iowa neurologist, noted that he had encountered patients who demonstrated the unfortunate habit of reversing words and other dyslexic-type problems. One of the most recent definitions of the term has been compiled by Theodore Harris and Richard Hodges in the International Reading Association publication, *A Dictionary of Reading and Related Terms.*[21] The medical profession tends to regard it as a disease for which there is some causative reason, whereas the psychological profession believes it is a serious problem which does not have a precise origin. Reading educators appear between these two positions.

There are numerous techniques involved in the diagnosis of dyslexia. Several of these strategies make extensive use of data obtained from observation of the student at work, while many reading specialists and school psychologists utilize formal commercial instruments to evaluate any dyslexic tendencies. A recent study by Hardman[22] noted that several widely known reading and psychological tests could be utilized by para-professionals to serve as screening devices for the differential diagnosis of dyslexia. Some of the tests are the *Slossen Intelligence Test, Peabody Picture Vocabulary Test, Wepman Auditory Discrimination Test,* and the *Gillespie Analysis Profile.*

In recent decades numerous approaches have been used to help alleviate the difficulties of dyslexic conditions. These include the VAKT (visual, auditory, kinesthetic and tactile) advocated by Kirk and the Fernald method created by Grace Fernald in the late 1920s. More recently, Rosengrant[23] conducted research and concluded that the microcomputer had the inherent capability to provide visual, auditory, and motor modes of support for students with dyslexic symptoms. Haddad and others[24] studied the common visual problems exhibited by dyslexics and which orthoptic exercises should be initiated. They found these students possessed numerous visual problems and that various orthoptic exercises such as framing, anti-suppression, and fusional exercises helped these learners to make measurable growth in the basic areas of reading skill development. Secondary educators should keep in mind that the technique(s) used depends on the chronological age of the learner, teacher preference, and the preferred learning style of the student. An eclectic approach under the direction of a team of teachers, school psychologists, medical officials, and school administrators should be instituted for the treatment of adolescent dyslexics.

Hyperactivity

Hyperactivity may be an indicator of some type of brain dysfunction and must be dealt with in a direct, planned manner. Zintz and Maggart[25] characterize hyperactivity as a higher-than-normal level of activity that is chronic in nature and is often characterized by distractability, emotional instability, poor social skills, and inability to adjust to environmental changes.

Many of these students tend to have a low tolerance level for any type of frustration or disruption, may be aggressive on occasion, and are prone to have a short attention span. In some instances, learners are placed in special environments with teachers who are specially trained to manage classroom environments where many hyperactive adolescents are present. For some students who are especially severe, the administration of various prescription drugs such as Ritalin, amphetamines, and thorazine may be helpful in some instances. Research data from numerous recent studies appear to suggest results that are inconclusive. On some occasions, the medicines achieve a positive result during which time the student is calmed and he or she is more receptive to instruction. A few limitations are noted with some adolescents due to undesirable side effects.

In summary, a significant percentage of disabled readers may be afflicted with neurological difficulties. Students who are so affected should be identified and instructed with methods and procedures to help in the maximum achievement of reading skills.

INTELLECTUAL LEVELS AND READING ABILITY

There appears to be a relatively high correlation between overall intelligence and reading ability, especially at the secondary and adult levels. The method of assessing intelligence is quite important, since the group tests at the primary level are more pictorial in nature and require little if any actual reading. Above the fourth grade level the items on intelligence measures are composed in printed form, and thus, the ability to read has a positive relationship to the final score regarding intelligence quotients. Margaret Early[26] emphasizes that non-verbal tests of intelligence also correlate highly with reading at advanced levels where the reading measure focuses more on comprehension than word recognition. Most students who read poorly in secondary schools also have problems comprehending oral language involving no reading.

The assessment of intelligence of a secondary learner is best achieved through the administration of an individual test such as the *Wechsler Adult Intelligence Scale* or the *Revised Stanford-Binet Intelligence Scale.* The examiner can make a careful analysis of both verbal and performance tasks and make judgments regarding the nature of high and low scores and how they relate to the act of reading. The performance section is especially important, since those items do not depend on direct reading experience and provide significant insights regarding overall intelligence. Many times, there is a great disparity between verbal and performance scores. A high performance score and an average or below average verbal result may suggest that the learner has potential for remediation of many existing reading problems. If the learner exhibits much difficulty with certain subtests such as Digit Span and Vocabulary, the prospects for long-term remediation may be restricted.

It is important to plan remedial programs after determining if the student is a **disabled** and/or a **retarded reader.** A **retarded reader** is one who is reading at a performance level below enrolled grade level, whereas a **disabled reader** is one reading below his/her level of potential reading level when taking into consideration intelligence quotient and number of years of school attended. Two reading authorities, Bond and Tinker,[27] constructed a reading expectancy formula in which they assume that the IQ is, in one respect, an index of learning and therefore the reading potential of a student can be calculated by multiplying the individual's IQ times the number of years in school (not counting kindergarten) and adding the number 1.0. (For example, if Mark has an IQ of 150 and is at the beginning of the tenth grade, he should be reading at an **estimated** 14.5 grade level.)

There are hundreds of disabled secondary readers in the content classrooms of America whose IQ levels are 120 or above, but since they can usually read at or above grade level they do not receive special reading instruction. These students need to have a specific curriculum to help them reach their full potential. Students with lesser potential may need an entirely different instruction. In a few instances, a well-designed plan of studies may actually be a factor in raising a given learner's IQ level because of overall improvement in vocabulary and general knowledge.

One group of authorities[28] warn, however, that some secondary teachers tend to view intelligence test scores as static figures; they have high expectations for students with high intelligence test scores and lower expectations for students with low scores. The intelligence test score may become a self-fulfilling prophecy for the student, thus IQ scores should be put in perspective and considered along with other factors.

SUMMARY

A significant number of secondary students cannot read at a satisfactory level and thus present serious curriculum and instructional problems for many instructors. One must remember to accept and treat a student's reading and learning abilities where they are at the present time without blaming elementary teachers, lack of phonics, or home conditions for the situation.

As much as possible, teachers need to try to understand and analyze all of the possible factors that may impact on the reading strengths and limitations of any one learner. As noted in this chapter these aspects may include emotional conditions, socioeconomic factors, physical aspects, previous educational experiences, neurological factors, and general intelligence. There is usually **not** a single cause for reading retardation. A careful analysis of the case studies of most problem readers indicates as many as three or four factors that created the disability.

Each secondary teacher should be aware of the limiting factors that impact on a given learner and design a reading skills curriculum that will meet his or her needs as closely as possible. Precise lessons dealing with skill improvement in word-attack, vocabulary, comprehension, and study skills can be found in the next several chapters.

REFERENCES

1. Howards, Melvin. *Reading Diagnosis and Instruction, An Integrated Approach.* Reston, Virginia, Reston Publishing Company, 1980, p. 153.
2. Ibid., p. 153.
3. Harris, Albert J. and Edward R. Sipay. *How to Increase Reading Ability* (*Eighth Edition*). New York, Longman, 1985, p. 313.

4. Dechant, Emerald V. *Improving the Teaching of Reading* (Third Edition). Englewood Cliffs, Prentice-Hall, 1982, p. 79.

5. Bond, Guy L., Miles A. Tinker and Barbara Wasson. *Reading Difficulties, Their Diagnosis and Correction* (Fourth Edition). Englewood Cliffs, Prentice-Hall, 1979, p. 101.

6. Zintz, Miles V. and Zelda R. Maggart. *The Reading Process, the Teacher and the Learner* (Fourth Edition). Dubuque, Wm. C. Brown, 1984, p. 445.

7. Miller, Wilma H. *The First R Elementary Reading Today.* Prospect Heights, Illinois, Waveland Press, 1983, p. 15.

8. Bates, Gary W. and Sally L. Navin, "Effects of Parent Counseling on Remedial Readers' Attitudes and Achievement." *Journal of Reading,* Vol. 30, No. 3 (December, 1986), pp. 254–257.

9. Callaway, Byron, Bob Jerrolds and Wayne Gwaltney, "The Relationship Between Reading and Language Achievement and Certain Sociological and Adjustment Factors." *Reading Improvement* (Spring, 1974), pp. 19–26.

10. Commission on Reading. *Becoming A Nation of Readers: The Report of the Commission on Reading.* Washington, D.C., The National Institute of Education, 1984, p. 57.

11. Snides, William, "Computer Use Grows in Chapter 1 Classes, New Report Finds." *Education Week,* Vol. 6, Number 33 (May 13, 1987) p. 15.

12. Montague, William, "Senate Gives Nod to More E. D. Funds." *Education Week,* Vol. 6, Number 33 (May 13, 1987), p. 14.

13. Burmeister, Lon E. *Reading Strategies for Secondary School Teachers.* Reading, Massachusetts, Addison-Wesley, 1976, p. 20.

14. LaPointe, Archie, "The State of Instruction in Reading and Writing in U.S. Elementary Schools." *Phi Delta Kappa* V. 68, No. 2 (October, 1986), pp. 138–138.

15. Commission on Reading, *Becoming a Nation of Readers,* p. 119.

16. Ibid., pp. 117–118.

17. Brown, R.E. "Teacher Skill and Other Variables Associated With Effectiveness in Teaching Reading." Unpublished dissertation, University of Indiana, 1978.

18. Bettelheim, Bruno and Karen Zelan. *On Learning To Read.* New York, Alfred A. Knopf, 1982, p. 220.

19. Dykstra, Robert, "The Effectiveness of Code- and Meaning-Emphasis Beginning Reading Programs." *The Reading Teacher,* Vol. 22 (April, 1968), pp. 17–23.

20. Pearson, P. David (Editor). *Handbook of Reading Research.* New York, Longman, 1984, p. 594.

21. Harris, Theodore L. and Richard E. Hodges (Co-Editors). *A Dictionary of Reading and Related Terms.* Newark, International Reading Association, 1981, p. 85.

22. Hardman, Patricia K., "The Training of Psycho-Educational Techniques (Paraprofessionals) to Administer a Screening Battery Which Delineates Dyslexia and Hyperkenesis." *Journal of Learning Disabilities,* 17, (October, 1984), p. 453.

23. Rosengrant, Teresa, "Using The Microcomputer As A Tool for Learning to Read and Write." *Journal of Learning Disabilities,* 18 (February, 1985), pp. 113–115.

24. Haddad, Heskel M. and others, "The Use of Orthoptics in Dyslexia." *Journal of Learning Disabilities,* 17 (March, 1984), pp. 142–144.
25. Zintz, Miles V. and Zelda R. Maggart. *Corrective Reading* (Fifth Edition). Dubuque, Iowa, Wm C. Brown, 1986, p. 485.
26. Early, Margaret. *Reading to Learn in Grades 5 to 12.* New York, Harcourt Brace Jovanovich, 1984, p. 70.
27. Bond, Guy l., Miles A. Tinker, and Barbara B. Wasson, *Reading Difficulties,* p. 62.
28. Roe, Betty D., Barbara D. Stoodt, and Paul C. Burns. *Secondary School Reading Instruction, The Content Areas.* Boston, Houghton Mifflin, 1987, p. 450.

Chapter III

PROMOTING WORD–ATTACK AND VOCABULARY SKILLS FOR ALL SECONDARY STUDENTS

This chapter and the chapters that follow are designed to provide important data and information relating to the basic skill segments of the reading process. A wide range of practical, classroom-tested teaching practices are provided to allow teachers to select those strategies that seem most applicable for his or her classroom. The procedure selected will depend naturally on a number of various factors, including class enrollment, student competencies, financial and physical resources available, and the preferred learning styles of the students involved.

Certainly one of the most important skills to be developed in strengthening reading competency is that of pronouncing words correctly and understanding their meanings in a number of different contexts. Unfortunately, far too many students reach the secondary level of learning and still lack the basic understanding of the fundamental principles of phonics, strategies for analyzing words structurally, knowledge of the meaning of words in various contexts, and the proper use of different types of dictionaries. One or more of the factors listed and discussed in the previous chapter may be responsible for the deficiencies.

Secondary classroom teachers should keep in mind that word attack is the center of the act of reading, and those students who have difficulties with this skill must be provided immediate and long-term assistance to overcome the problem. Some secondary administrators report that there may be as many as 75 to 80 percent of all students with pronunciation difficulties.

The development of one's vocabulary is necessary and essential if satisfactory reading growth is to be realized in such vital areas as silent reading comprehension and oral and written language and communication. The enlargement of a reader's vocabulary is a **lifelong** process, and each and every secondary teacher of content subjects must assume a significant responsibility for helping learners reach a maximum level of growth in the listening, speaking, reading, and writing vocabularies. This chapter is devoted to providing vital information and suggestions for teachers in building developmental, remedial, and corrective reading programs in these two important areas.

To accomplish the preceding goal, the following four major topics are included in this chapter: the importance and nature of word-attack skills; procedures for strengthening word-attack skills; types of vocabulary; and strategies for building and evaluating vocabulary skills. A summary and a body of references conclude the chapter.

THE IMPORTANCE AND NATURE OF WORD-ATTACK SKILLS

In analyzing the processes involved in the physical and mental processes of reading, the first and foremost task for the reader is that of identifying and perceiving the printed symbols which stand for the spoken sounds — in other words grasping the true relationships existing between graphemes and morphemes. In the very first stage of reading the perceiver has the feeling or awareness that something is present, that it is related to some kind of symbol or word, and that understanding or meaning is a natural end product of the act of reading.[1]

The alert, normal, preschool child is capable of saying literally hundreds of words that he or she has heard spoken by parents and other adults. Developing the capability to locate and decode words is his or her most immediate responsibility. During the past several decades reading specialists have determined through various research studies that the sequential and systematic development of major decoding strategies is vital if the learner is to understand the word-attack process. At the secondary level, the most important of these tools are phonetic analysis, structural analysis, use of the dictionary, and context clues.

There have been many educational debates and discussions among educators relating to the method or strategy that should be utilized with all learners. Particularly vocal have been those persons who advocate a certain brand or kind of phonics program as the sure, ultimate procedure for unlocking words. Due to the fact that a high percentage (86%) of the words of the English language can be attacked by a phonetic principle, these methods must not be diminished in their importance. However, the 14 percent of the words that cannot be analyzed through phonic methods constitute some of the most common words in daily language such as the word "one." These and other words must be attacked by secondary students by utilizing a multiple approach to word analysis that includes the use of sight words, context clues, and structural analysis. In other words, the proficient reader makes simultaneous use of a variety of tools. He or she may note in the word "unfaithful" that there are three meaning units—the prefix "un", the root word "faith", and the suffix "ful." Since most students can pronounce and understand the meanings of most prefixes and suffixes, the only remaining segment of the word to be considered is the root word "faith."

The adolescent recalls that the letter "f" is a consonant and the vast majority of these letters have a regular sound. Elementary teachers have taught and provided skill lessons dealing with vowel digraphs and the attendant principle that the first vowel is sounded and the second one is silent in most cases. With this concept in mind, the learner attaches the long sound to the "a" and proceeds to pronounce "faith" as "faith." Further, he or she notes that the "ful" suffix contains a schwa or unaccented vowel sound. Placing all of the elements together—the prefix, the sounds of the letters in the root word, and the suffix—the reader is then able to pronounce the word correctly.

There are numerous techniques and strategies that one can implement on a continuous and regular basis for evaluating word-attack skills such as examining the results of vocabulary tests taken from commercial instruments. Teachers should remember that, at best, reading tests take a sampling of students' knowledge of vocabulary, for instance, and their ability to recognize "right" answers after reading a passage which may or may not treat a subject that is familiar to them.[2] The administration of teacher-made informal tests such as those found later in this chapter can also be valuable. Clues regarding certain kinds of word-attack difficulties can be gathered from listening carefully to how the student pronounces various words during class discussions.

The Role of Phonics in Secondary Reading

If the secondary reader has been exposed to a well-developed reading skills program at the elementary school level, he or she has no doubt mastered the basic elements of phonics, and thus the vast majority of upper grade and secondary students will probably need only a brief review over some of the principles they have learned. Phonetic analysis is used to a very limited degree at the secondary level due to the fact that structural analysis and context clues are the basic tools employed.

There are some situations that present themselves in content lessons that make it possible for a secondary teacher to reinforce phonic skills.

1. During the presentation of the new vocabulary words in a given unit, emphasize how various words contain phonic elements and how these blend together to form new words.

2. Using a practice sheet, list some of the special words and phrases used in the lesson or unit to be studied. Ask students to divide the words into syllables and place appropriate phonetic markings such as a breve or macron where they belong above the letters with short and long vowel sounds.

3. Call attention to the glossary and any specialized dictionaries related to the area and explain the meanings of various phonetic markings.

Structural Analysis and the Secondary Reading Process

Structural analysis involves the use of various word parts such as prefixes, suffixes, root words, and syllables that are joined together to form compound words to help in the identification of unfamiliar words. This technique is extremely helpful in the analysis of content words, since there are numerous words which contain word parts and appear repeatedly in a given discipline.[3] Science and social studies print materials contain an unusually large variety of multisyllabic words. In examining a short selection of a general science textbook, one may find such words as *irreversible, pharmacology, immeasurable, medicinally, hydrometer, parasympathetic, microbicide, nephritis,* and *segmentation.* Because these words are significant to the overall understanding of the topics presented, the secondary instructor must help each student pronounce and derive meanings for each of these and similar words. Explanations need to be made regarding the importance of affixes, root words, and inflectional endings and how these combine to form a useful word. Learners should understand that the basic meaning of any multisyllabic words is found in the root or base word and that various inflectional endings such as *es, ing, est,* and *er* merely alter the refined meaning of the word.

Instruction regarding the function of affixes needs to be undertaken to demonstrate how the meaning of a base word may be changed. The following pairs of words are common examples of how certain affixes affect word meaning: *paint — repaint; microbe — microbes; arm — disarm;*

ordinary—extraordinary; and *practice—malpractice.* Direct teaching must be undertaken to help secondary students gain a complete understanding of certain affixes, their meanings, and appropriate examples. The following is a table of examples of affixes with invariant meanings that may be utilized in any content area.

AFFIX	MEANING	EXAMPLE
1. hydro	water	hydrosphere
2. mono	one	monoplane
3. phono	sound	phonograph
4. poly	many	polygon
5. mis	wrong	mistake
6. bility	quality of being	mobility
7. cide	destroying of	germicide
8. graph	writing or recording	polygraph
9. scope	instrument for detecting	microscope
10. ful	fullness or abundance	beautiful

With regard to inflectional endings and root words, each secondary student should have a thorough understanding of several basic principles with regard to structural analysis. As needed, these should be reviewed with groups of students and appropriate competency evaluations conducted to help assure that they are a part of the knowledge base of the learner.

1. If a root word ends with the letter "e," the "e" is dropped when an ending that begins with a vowel is added: (*take, taking*).

2. If a syllable or word ends in a single consonant preceded by a vowel, the consonant is often doubled when an ending is added: (map, mapped; net, netted)

3. Numerous words can be formed by merely adding an inflectional ending with no change in the root word (picked, girls, masking, watches).

4. In situations where a word ends with the letter "y" preceded by a consonant, the "y" is normally changed to an "i" before an ending is added: (manliness, fatalities). If the "y" is preceded by a vowel, there is usually no change in the root word when an ending is added: (ploys, bays).

5. Words that end in "f" or "fe" often form their plurals by changing the "f" to a "v" and adding the plural endings: (knives, scarves).

Due to the fact that there is much attention given to syllabication as a part of an overall program of structural analysis instruction, several basic principles should be reviewed and understood by all secondary students.

1. Every syllable encountered in any recognizable common or proper word must contain either a vowel **or** vowel sound: (in, Srb).

2. If a word contains a prefix and root word, the word is usually divided between the two meaning units: (unable, mistake).

3. When two consonants are preceded and followed by a vowel, the word is normally divided into syllables after the first vowel that is usually long: (be-hind, mi-ler, or mo-tel).

4. If a word ends in a consonant with the letters "le" at the end, the word is divided before the consonant: (ma-ple, pur-ple, ap-ple).

5. When two consonants are surrounded by two vowels, the word is normally separated into syllables between the two consonants with the first vowel retaining a short sound (of-ten, mop-per).

Analyzing Words in Various Contexts

One of the most common means of unlocking words at the secondary level is the use of context clues. A context clue is when the student analyzes the *approximate* meaning of a word from a body of material and applies word-attack skills to the unknown word with the goal of attempting to discover if the word is in his speaking vocabulary. In many instances, the words in the body of the context will not provide a meaning clue; thus, the reader is forced to depend on the dictionary as a final source of information.

One must remember that relying only on context, however, is more appropriate for good readers who are at the upper grade and secondary levels. Teachers must be careful not to assume that everyone will understand new concepts simply because they have been used in written context.[4] The technique is only valuable if the reader has an adequate background of knowledge and possesses efficient decoding skills.

Generally speaking, all types of context clues can be grouped into two major divisions: syntactical or structural tools and format or typographical strategies. The former group involves the use of synonyms, antonyms, and appositives and various cause-effect relationships. The latter facet deals with various textbook features such as the glossary, reference sections, underlined and italicized words and phrases, and footnotes of various kinds.

There are eight types or kinds of context clues that are generally found in most reading material. They are as follows:

1. **Summary.** (The unknown word or phrase outlines the ideas that precede it.)

Example: The several houses that were destroyed in the tornado represented a major **calamity** for the owners involved.

2. **Association.** (The unfamiliar word is associated or related to a known word.)

Example: He ran the race and won easily with the **preciseness** of a true champion.

3. **Contrast** (The unknown word has a meaning opposite of the known word.)

Example: He was the father of the tribe while she was the **matriarch.**

4. **Precise Description.** (The unfamiliar word is defined directly in the sentence.)

Example: The ugly, frightful animal was indeed a very **hideous** creature.

5. **Mood Reflection.** (The unknown words correlate with a mood or feeling which has been built into the sentence.)

Example: The disrespectful people in the church service gave us the idea that they were very **irreverent.**

6. **Restatement.** (The unfamiliar word is explained in the statement.)

Example: The **omniscient** person appeared to have complete and infinite knowledge about the entire field of chemistry.

7. **Experience Background.** (The unknown word's meaning can be derived by using the reader's background of experience.)

Example: At the dance several **minuets** were played for those who wanted to dance slowly and stately.

8. **Inference.** (The meaning of the word can be derived in light of the reader's familiarity with everyday expressions.)

Example: When I was in the hospital, the nurse had me swallow different kinds of **medications.**

In a later section there are examples of classroom exercises that can be used to build context clue efficiency.

Proper Use of Dictionaries

Even though secondary students have been exposed to numerous dictionaries during their elementary school experiences, many of them lack the necessary skills to find a particular word, determine how it should be pronounced, and select the correct meaning for some defined syntactical structure. If a student is to be successful in using a dictionary, a number of skills and understandings need to be developed according to Heilman, Blair, and Rupley. Some of them are: (a) knowledge of alphabetical order; (b) a word may have different meanings; (c) knowledge of root words and inflected and derived words; and (d) the sound values of different letters.[5]

By the time a student has reached the secondary level, he or she should be able to use appropriate alphabetical knowledge to find a word and derive the correct way to pronounce the word and select its precise meaning for a given context. In order for upper grade and secondary students to accomplish this goal, the teacher should have a variety of levels of dictionaries as resources. Early notes that high school English curricula should feature at least one unit on the history and uses of dictionaries, and a wide sampling of modern and early versions should be available from the media center. Every classroom should have six dictionaries of different levels to allow students to check shades of meaning and verify their guesses based on content.[6]

The dictionary helps a student to find the precise meaning of a word as well as its correct pronunciation. Many learners need help in choosing the **one** meaning that fits a particular context. Most dictionaries incorporate multiple meanings for words which creates a problem for the student. With appropriate practice most learners can learn how to use the content to select the correct meaning. The thesaurus may also be helpful as a device for understanding the meanings of words. There are some students who prefer the thesaurus, since they find it easier to understand and remember synonyms than dictionary definitions.[7]

Teachers should exercise care in choosing the words that are selected for study in a dictionary. The words should be those that represent key concepts and are vital to the overall understanding of a topic. Long lists of exotic and/or little-used words should be avoided. Learners should be motivated to enlarge their overall reading, speaking, and writing vocabularies through systematic, regular use of the dictionary and thesaurus.

PROCEDURES FOR STRENGTHENING WORD–ATTACK SKILLS

As noted in the previous sections, secondary readers make use of a variety of word-attack strategies to analyze words which are unknown to them. These include phonic analysis, structural analysis, context clues, and the dictionary and/or thesaurus. On a selected basis related to student need, the instructor should formulate lesson plans to help each learner improve efficiency in each skill area. The suggested lessons are merely representative of the multitude of teacher-generated strategies that could be utilized. (It is important to remember to utilize the exercises for those who have a *demonstrated* limitation in a particular skill. Students who are excellent readers and have little, if any, deficiency in this area should be excused from the lessons.) There are certain kinds of commercial materials that may be useful for skill building in word analysis.

I. Phonic Skill Lessons

To evaluate a given learner's ability to recognize phonic elements the following lesson may be constructed and marked as requested.

A. *Directions:* Circle the consonant digraph or vowel digraph in each of these words.

1. thick	5. saw	9. snow
2. shout	6. food	10. telephone
3. taught	7. rough	11. sing
4. chicken	8. look	12. took

B. *Directions:* Circle the consonant blend in each of the following words.

1. crop	5. strong	9. step
2. close	6. sweep	10. skunk
3. crank	7. spoke	11. frigid
4. scrimp	8. flip	12. clock

C. *Directions.* Each word contains a short or long vowel sound. Write "short" or "long" on the blank before each word.

_____	1. end	_____	5. trip	_____	9. cab
_____	2. me	_____	6. city	_____	10. fist
_____	3. mate	_____	7. chap	_____	11. tree
_____	4. mit	_____	8. meat	_____	12. it

II. Structural Analysis Lessons

A. *Directions.* Many words in the English language contain *affixes* such as *prefixes* placed at the beginning of a root word and suffixes that are placed at the end of a root word. Examples of affixes are "ish," "er," "ous," "co," "mis," "trans," "pre," "un," and "de." Add an affix to each of the following words to form a new word. Use each new word in a sentence.

1. mit _____ _____
2. plain _____ _____
3. claim _____ _____
4. enlarge _____ _____
5. loud _____ _____
6. condition _____ _____
7. protect _____ _____
8. tied _____ _____
9. pretend _____ _____
10. protect _____ _____

B. *Directions.* Each of the following sentences contains a blank for a new word that should be added to complete the sentence. Add an affix to the word to the left of each sentence. Write the word on the blank.

treat   1. He was unkind to the dog and often _____ it.
fool   2. It was _____ for him to swim in deep water.
vest   3. To make money, you might _____ in the stock market.
pare   4. Always _____ for the work you are to do.
master   5. The organist gave a _____ performance.
handled   6. The player _____ the ball.
owner   7. He was the _____ of the car.
danger   8. It is _____ to drive a car with worn tires.

C. *Directions.* Find a word in the second list which goes with a word in the first list to form a compound word. Write the word on the blank following the first word.

List 1		List 2
1. broad	_____	with
2. drop	_____	weight
3. forth	_____	out
4. goal	_____	cap
5. heavy	_____	sider
6. ice	_____	weed
7. knock	_____	side
8. out	_____	keeper
9. milk	_____	put
10. shot	_____	forge

D. *Directions.* Many words in the English language have derived forms. Study the various nouns listed below. Write three derived words on the blanks which follow. The first one is done for you.

1. etch	etched	etcher	etching
2. bang			
3. heave			
4. infect			
5. meet			
6. nod			
7. peal			
8. pull			
9. segregate			
10. slump			

III. Context Clues Skills Lessons

As noted earlier, the typical secondary and/or adult reader makes significant use of context clues to arrive at the approximate meaning of a given word. The following exercises represent some ideas for compiling appropriate practice lessons for building this important skill.

A. *Directions.* There are many words in the English language that look very similar. A change or switch of one or more letters can change the entire meaning of the word. It is important to examine each word carefully to see if the spelling of the word fits the context where it is found. Below are ten sentences. Each sentence contains a misused word. Locate the word and write the word on the first blank following the sentence. On the second blank, write the word you think should go in its place.

1. The wide prairie represented a huge expense of land.

    _____ _____

2. The desert was served at the end of the meal.

    _____ _____

3. That is no execute for being late to class.

    _____ _____

4. The intrigue design of the basket was complete with many twists and turns that were very complicated.

    _____ _____

5. Persons who work in vegetable fields are commonly thought of as migrate workers.

    _____ _____

6. Mrs. Brown baked a cheery pie for the church picnic.

_____ _____

7. The county fare was complete with rides, games, and exhibits.

_____ _____

8. One should always sink a song at the right pitch.

_____ _____

9. My favorite fruit is a pare.

_____ _____

10. Most people eat serial for breakfast.

_____ _____

B. *Directions.* The following is a short selection in which every fifth word has been left out. There are three words at the close of the story for each blank. Select the best word for each of the blanks.

Abraham Lincoln was elected (1) in November of 1860. (2) inauguration took place in (3) , 1861. During this period (4) history, several states (5) to secede from the (6) . Seven states eventually seceded (7) formed the Confederate States (8) America. The president of (9) Confederacy was Jefferson Davis. (10) former senator from Mississippi. (11) afterward, the Civil War (12) with the attack on Fort (13) . There were a number of (14) causes for the war. (15) North and South had (16) kinds of people, land, (17) climate. The Southern states (18) mostly agriculture while the (19) states engaged in trade (20) industry.

1. nearly	President	twice
2. people	one	his
3. March	late	upper
4. of	the	early
5. tripped	moved	enlarged
6. kingdom	history	nation
7. and	two	nearly
8. the	of	relative
9. any	Northern	the
10. a	the	twice
11. lately	soon	in
12. was	big	began
13. Sumter	Kansas	hill
14. of	three	huge

15. numerous	a	the
16. different	pretty	poor
17. but	and	what
18. were	recently	congregated
19. Northern	Western	under
20. with	and	the

IV. Dictionary Skills Lessons

The following lessons are designed to provide additional practice for all students in the skill of using the dictionary in a more appropriate manner. Those students who score at less than an 80 percent level of accuracy should receive individualized instruction in those areas which need strengthening.

A. *Directions.* You have been provided with a class dictionary. Below are five statements with underlined words. Following the sentences are three pairs of guide words from three pages in the dictionary. Write the number of the page where the underlined word would be found.

1. The hickory is a North American tree in the same family as the walnut. (a) page 283, hibernate—highland; (b) page 284, highlander—hinder; (c) page 285, hindermost—history.

2. That old man is very eccentric. (a) page 120, earache—easily; (b) page 121, easiness—eatable; (c) page 122, eaten—echidna.

3. The cowboy used a goad for driving the cattle to the pasture. (a) page 134, gnomic—goat; (b) page 135, goatee—golden; (c) page 136, goldfish—goodish.

4. The piano player gave a masterful performance during the entire concert. (a) page 389, marquise—martyr; (b) page 390, martyrdom—massive; (c) massy—mastic. 5. He forbid me from going to the circus. (a) page 149, folio—football; (b) page 150, footgear—forage; (c) page 151, foray—foreclose.

B. *Directions.* There are thousands of words in the English language and many of the words have several meanings. When you see a word in a sentence, you need to select the correct meaning of the word. In the following lesson are several definitions of a word, a sentence in which the word is used, and a multiple-choice item to test to see if you can choose the definition for the word. Circle the number of the *correct* answer for each item.

Ligature   (1) Anything used to bind up something such as a cord.
            (2) A group of musical notes connected by a slur.
            (3) Two or three letters joined in printing.
The packages should be bound with a ligature.
Ligature in the above sentence refers to:
            (1) Definition No. 1.
            (2) Definition No. 2.
            (3) Definition No. 3.

Perspective (1) Art of drawing objects on a level surface
                  to show distance.
            (2) Effect of length of time of events on the mind.
            (3) The view in front of something.
The things that happened to me last year seem not so serious when observed in perspective.
Perspective in the above sentence refers to:
            (1) Definition No. 1.
            (2) Definition No. 2.
            (3) Definition No. 3.

C. *Directions.* Many words in the English language can be written as either singular or plural words. Read the sentences below and find the underlined words using your dictionary. Write the plural form for the underlined word on the blank at the end of the sentence.

1. We had an *offertory* during our church service.
   _____

2. The army *infantry* was sent to battle the enemy.
   _____

3. The *family* went to the picnic last Sunday.
   _____

4. A large *rostrum* was built for the speaker.
   _____

5. The professor conducted a *seminar*.
   _____

D. *Directions.* Locating words in the dictionary is easy if you know how to alphabetize words in their proper order. Look carefully at the three words in each of the following groups. Write the words and put them in their **proper** alphabetical order.

experienced	_____	harmony	_____
expensive	_____	harpist	_____
experience	_____	harness	_____
octoroon	_____	revery	_____
octopus	_____	reversion	_____
ocular	_____	revert	_____
gauntlet	_____	obsolete	_____
gantlet	_____	obsolescent	_____
gaunt	_____	obstacle	_____

E. *Directions.* The following words are inflected forms of certain root or base words. Study the words in your dictionary and write the root or base word on the blank following each word.

expensive	_____	plugger	_____
loveless	_____	revolved	_____
motivation	_____	scrabbling	_____
openness	_____	staring	_____

In addition to the several suggested exercises above, many publishers of dictionaries sell lesson booklets that correlate with the style and nature of their particular dictionaries. There are other commercial lesson series such as those from Trillium Press (Box 209, Monroe, New York 10950), entitled *Vocabulary Skills Mastery Kits* by Donald C. Cushenbery.

TYPES OF VOCABULARY

One of the most important goals of any viable secondary curriculum should be that of helping each learner develop the five general types of vocabulary (listening, speaking, reading, writing, and potential) at a maximum rate. Each of these types increase at a reasonably steady rate if certain positive factors are in evidence such as a satisfactory level of intelligence, student motivation, and appropriate interaction with fellow students, teachers, family members, and persons in the society in general. A conscious and direct effort must be exerted by each instructor for helping each student build these vocabularies.

Listening Vocabulary

Shortly after birth, the normal human being starts the acquisition of a basic listening vocabulary. The young learner listens carefully to the various phonemes in the word C–A–T and gradually associates them as a unit to mean a small furry animal that purrs. Dialect and various speaking patterns are developed as a result of the imitation of the way words and sentences are spoken by parents, siblings, and others who are in his/her immediate environment. If the words are spoken repeatedly in a proper context, a high level of listening vocabulary may be established. The degree and amount of listening vocabulary attained depends quite naturally on the type and nature of the child's environment. If the boy or girl is reared in an environment where little conversation takes place, the level of the listening environment will be quite limited. It is urgent for parents to understand the importance of speaking naturally and frequently to the child, since a large amount of oral expression forms the basis for constructing all of the other types of vocabulary. Inviting the young child to repeat what has been said helps to enlarge the speaking vocabulary.

Throughout life, the amount or kind of words in one's listening vocabulary is far larger than the number of words attributed to the speaking and writing vocabularies. The degree of the listening vocabulary as noted earlier is highly dependent on the environment. Two authorities who have made studies in the area of vocabulary estimate that the typical middle-class, six-year-old child may have as many as 8,000 to 10,000 words in the listening vocabulary.[8] Children who have been raised in a particularly stimulating environment may exhibit a listening vocabulary as high as 12,000 to 14,000 words. Assessment procedures for determining such data are imprecise; thus exact figures are difficult to determine.

Speaking Vocabulary

The construction of a speaking vocabulary is directly related to the nature of the listening vocabulary that has been established. If the learner has had the good fortune of living in a home environment where many oral comments and conversations have been provided, there is a greater prospect of developing an effective level of speaking proficiency. On the other hand, a student who has encountered a deprived environment will no doubt have a very limited speaking vocabulary. Young children with advantaged environments and an above average level of intelligence may be able to demonstrate a speaking vocabulary of hundreds of words.

The influence of the teacher's instruction has a positive impact on speaking vocabulary levels. Secondary instructors who motivate students to learn, introduce new vocabulary words systematically, and encourage oral discussion and reports can do much to increase speaking efficiency. Accordingly, many opportunities should be given for each learner to make oral contributions in a number of teaching-learning environments. Teachers should model much appropriate oral language which acquaints older students with a variety of new words. Hopefully, many learners will imitate and attempt to remember many new words that add to the speaking vocabulary.

Students can be apprised of their current strengths and limitations in the area of speaking vocabulary by having them listen and/or view videotapes and audiotapes of oral speaking assignments. Proper attention can be given to certain corrections which may be needed with regard to the correct pronunciation of certain words. Evaluation can be also made of strengths and limitations in semantic structure of sentences.

Reading Vocabulary

If very young children have not been enrolled in preschools where formal reading instruction is undertaken, they have probably had little opportunity to build a substantial reading vocabulary. The basis for enlarging reading vocabulary entails the use and implementation of various word-attack tools such as phonics and structural analysis. One may assume that those words that are a part of a learner's reading vocabulary have already been made a part of his or her listening and/or speaking vocabulary.

Many research studies suggest that a pupil's reading vocabulary is larger than the speaking vocabulary. The child's background of experience has a significant relationship to the overall level of reading vocabulary obtained. The present level of a secondary student's reading vocabulary can be evaluated through the use of both formal and informal reading tests. (Several of these are described later in this chapter.) Information gained from these instruments should be valuable to the secondary instructor for determining the nature and type of instruction which should be offered to help insure maximum growth in reading vocabulary.

Writing Vocabulary

One's writing vocabulary has no doubt the smallest inventory of any of the various vocabularies discussed previously. The average high school student may have the ability to listen and understand the meanings of numerous words; however, the words used in writing assignments may be quite restricted. Secondary teachers can help learners build a storehouse of words in his/her writing vocabulary through the use of many different types of creative writing exercises. As Pearce[9] notes, writing can most productively be viewed as one mode of language processing, along with listening, speaking, and reading. Anytime students can process information or communicate information and facts, then they can write. The writing of various learned vocabulary words can serve as a catalyst for further study and reflection on a topic as opposed to being an end in itself.

Potential Vocabulary

The term "potential vocabulary" refers to all of the words a given secondary student can understand when he or she is in a number of different situations or circumstances. The attachment of a large body of relevant affixes such as prefixes and suffixes to base words enables a reader to add a significant number of words to his or her potential vocabulary. Careful instruction in the use of semantic structure at the primary and intermediate grade levels may have a substantial impact on the eventual potential level achieved by secondary learners. There are a variety of methods that may be used by parents and instructors to help students become acquainted with a multitude of words. The references contain a large number of ideas with regard to print and electronics media that may be utilized for vocabulary enlargement. Special graded dictionaries that are published by established companies may also be quite helpful. Every opportunity should be given to provide media presentations such as films, filmstrips, and VCR tapes to help secondary students build potential vocabulary levels.

STRATEGIES FOR BUILDING AND EVALUATING VOCABULARY SKILLS

The following are seven sample exercises that may be helpful for use with secondary students in building overall vocabulary skill competencies. The exercises can be restructured to meet a particular student's grade level, interests, and other factors.

Exercise 1: Scrambled Words

Directions: Read the definition for each word and then unscramble the letters to form the word that corresponds to the definition. Write the word on the blank provided.

1. rseceles _____ Persons who cast their votes for the candidate of their political party.
2. siederntp _____ Considered the leader of the party in power.
3. ndmentemas _____ Known as the Bill of Rights to the Constitution.
4. ndiani _____ Name of tribes living in the <u>Louisiana</u> Territory.
5. totnoc ing _____ This was an important invention for harvesting a major Southern crop.
6. deceeds _____ What some states did during the Civil War.
7. avless _____ Name given to persons being held against their will.
8. iounn _____ Name of army who fought against the Confederate soldiers during the Civil War.

Exercise 2: Matching

Directions: Match the items in Column B with those in Column A.

1. The highest court level
2. Land purchased by President Jefferson
3. Making law void
4. Fee charged for trading
5. Segregation
6. Lynching
7. Monopoly
8. Assimilation

A. Nullification
B. Separation
C. Control by a single person or company
D. Louisiana Purchase
E. Tariff
F. Supreme Court
G. Becoming part of something
H. Hanging a person by a mob

Exercise 3: Find the Right Word

Directions: Below is a list of words. Select a word from the list and write it on the blanks in the sentences that follow:

planters	colonies
gold	secede
transportation	economic
national	regulations

1. Trade with Spanish _____ in South America had been regulated by Spanish authorities.
2. A small group of rich _____ took charge of southern politics.
3. Many northerners believed that no state had the right to _____ from the Union.
4. The Civil War brought many _____ changes.
5. Many people went to California in 1848 after _____ was discovered.
6. Better _____ brought new people to the region.
7. Government _____ limited the growth of business.
8. By 1840, a strong _____ pride existed.

Exercise 4: Matching Word Meanings

Directions: Look at the underlined word in each line. Study the four words that follow. Circle the word which means the same or nearly the same as the underlined word.

1. germinate	calculate	sprout	maximum	preface
2. possess	remove	effective	penchant	own
3. penetrate	enter	guidance	skewer	theology
4. mellow	tasty	soft	positive	reaction
5. fictitious	maximum	unreal	dealt	foresee
6. moot	morbid	forfeit	infer	debatable
7. lagoon	monsoon	pond	lacuna	maverick
8. shad	fish	kinescope	skein	lien
9. maximum	pulp	rocket	largest	pretend
10. shaft	neutral	particle	pyrite	arrow

Exercise 5: Using Analogies

Directions: There are many analogies in the English language. An analogy shows the relationship of one word to another. Study the following analogies and underline the word among the choices that complete the analogy.

1. black: white/day   (a) morning   (b) noon   (c) night
2. hot: summer/cold   (a) winter   (b) spring   (c) fall
3. peach: pear/maple   (a) tree   (b) oak   (c) brown
4. good: bad/health   (a) sickness   (b) strength   (c) body
5. little: big/calf   (a) cow   (b) animal   (c) milk
6. feat: feet/red   (a) blue   (b) color   (c) read

7. finger: hand/toe   (a) ankle   (b) bone   (c) foot
8. touchdown: football/goal   (a) hockey   (b) baseball   (c) golf
9. hat: head/shoes   (a) body   (b) feet   (c) health
10. lovely: beautiful/sad   (a) glad   (b) sorrow   (c) unhappy

Exercise 6: Supply the Missing Letters

Directions: The use of context clues to form new words is an important means of improving vocabulary. The following sentences contain words with missing letters. Fill in the missing letters to ensure that the sentences have meaning and make sense.

1. The f __ __ tball g __ __ e pro __ __ d to be ex __ __ ting but we won the co __ __ est.
2. There are n __ __ erous co __ __ uters at our sch __ __ l for use by te __ __ hers and st __ __ ents.
3. I was un __ __ epared for the dis __ __ action that pre __ __ ded the a __ __ ual pa __ __ de.
4. It is dis __ __ essing to en __ __ unter bo __ __ les that ca __ __ ot be o __ __ ned.
5. The nu __ __ rous b __ __ ks in the s __ __ ool li __ __ ary rep __ __ sent a we __ __ th of inf __ __ mation.
6. The co __ pu __ ters in our cl __ ssr __ __ m are to be u __ __ d by all st __ __ ents.
7. To re __ __ ive the best g __ __ des, re __ __ ires much t __ me and e __ __ ort.
8. Te __ __ hers can be of mu __ h help in pre __ __ ring st __ __ ents for the f __ __ ure.
9. We can i __ __ rove our re __ __ ing ski __ __ s by re __ __ ing and st __ __ ying re __ __ arly on ass __ __ nments.
10. Sh __ __ ing bo __ ks with ot __ __ rs is both fun and in __ __ resting.

Exercise 7: Finding Words With Prefixes

Directions: Many of the words that are added to one's speaking and writing vocabularies contain prefixes. Some of the common prefixes are *be* (by); *de* (from); *en* (in); *ex* (out); *im* (not); *ob* (away); *re* (back); and *super* (over). Each of the sentences contains one or more words with prefixes. Circle the words that contain a prefix.

1. **Because he was late, it was necessary to deduct his salary and be supervised by a fellow worker.**

2. Behind the giant sign, one could see an obstruction which prevented an exit from the arena.

3. The impure water restricted the type of drink that could be enjoyed by the tourists.

4. The best defense in basketball is to oppose the other team by engaging in a fast-paced game.

5. Some countries export more goods than they import.

6. The abnormal temperatures of the past week have caused us to be very uncomfortable.

7. One way to improve reading skills is by referring to previous experiences for reinforcement.

8. My supervisor explained the reasons why she could not attend the meeting.

Methods of Evaluating Vocabulary Skills

There are numerous formal and informal strategies for evaluating a student's level of vocabulary proficiency at the secondary level. Content teachers may use informal teacher-made evaluation devices to gain information relative to the level of word meaning. The following are some classroom-tested strategies that may be utilized in classes which make use of a significant amount of print media.

1. Construct a series of sentences, with each sentence containing a blank for the insertion of a key vocabulary word. List the words in a scrambled fashion at the bottom of the page. As students select a desired word, it should be crossed off the list.

2. Place a list of key words on the left side of the page. Place four definitions to the right of the key word. The one definition that is correct for the key word should be underlined. An accuracy score of at least 80 percent or more should be expected.

3. Key words and definitions are placed in scrambled order in two columns. Students should be asked to match the words with their correct definitions.

4. A cloze technique test may be employed. Using a 260 to 270-word passage of material from a required text, duplicate the first sentence intact. Beginning with the second sentence, leave a blank space for every fifth word until 50 blanks have been formed. Ask each student to complete the exercise by writing the most logical word for each blank. The exercise should be checked using the words from the original text as the

source for correctness of answers. A student's writing vocabulary may be considered adequate if he or she supplies at least 20 correct words for the 50 blanks.

In addition to the informal procedures just listed, there are several commercial standardized tests and systems that may be utilized. The following is a sample list of such items for use with secondary students.

1. *Comprehensive Tests of Basic Skills, Form V* (Publishers Test Service) has nine levels which evaluate several basic skills including reading, spelling, language, and reference skills. Levels J and K are intended for secondary students.

2. *Degrees of Reading Power* (Psychological Corporation) is a specialized program providing for both assessment and instruction in reading. Each form measures a wide range of reading ability and is useful for all kinds of secondary students including special education, gifted and talented, and ESL students.

3. *Iowa Silent Reading Tests* (Psychological Corporation) measure four major reading components including vocabulary and is designed for grades 6–12 and college.

4. *Nelson-Denny Reading Test* (Riverside) is intended for grades 9–12 and measures student competency with regard to vocabulary, comprehension, and rate of reading.

5. *Skills Bank* (CTB–McGraw-Hill) is a software system for Apple and IBM microcomputers. It provides help for students in many ways, including the reinforcement of test-taking skills. It covers all of the major skills included on nationally known achievement tests. One of the major components is vocabulary and includes lesson disks, a student disk, and a manual.

6. *Stanford Diagnostic Reading Test: Third Edition* (Psychological Corporation) measures three important reading segments. One of the domains is vocabulary (auditory vocabulary, vocabulary, word parts). The blue level is intended for grades 8.8 to 12.8.

7. *Test of Adolescent Language* (Publishers Test Service) contains eight subtests including vocabulary and seven others.

8. *Wide Range Achievement Test* (Publishers Test Service) may be used at all grade levels. The new norms provide for derived scores and grade estimates for all ages. The test is quickly administered in 15 to 30 minutes and can be hand-scored in less than five minutes.

9. *Test of Cognitive Skills* (CTB–McGraw-Hill) evaluates sequences, analogies, memory, and verbal reasoning.

10. *Testmate* (CTB–McGraw-Hill) is a new microcomputer software system that allows school systems to scan, score, and report test data from both norm-referenced and criterion-referenced tests in reading and other areas. It is capable of making numerous statistical analyses of test results.

SUMMARY

Word attack is a very important reading skill to develop since it is the heart of the reading act. There are numerous techniques one can use to pronounce words, including phonics, structural analysis, context clues, and the dictionary. The various teaching strategies that are described in this chapter are carefully planned for building word-attack proficiencies for secondary students.

Vocabulary development should be a continuous effort, and direct and specific lessons in all content areas should be conducted. Words which are unique to a given content area should be taught by the instructors teaching those classes. Sample lessons are included in the previous section that can be adapted for all subject lessons. Careful attention should be given to the evaluation of a given learner's level of vocabulary proficiency through the use of both informal and commercial tests and strategies. The data derived from these procedures should serve as the foundation for formulating appropriate lessons for further vocabulary development.

REFERENCES

1. Karlin, Robert. *Teaching Reading in High School.* New York, Harper and Row, 1984, p. 45.
2. Early, Margaret. *Reading to Learn in Grades 5 to 12.* New York, Harcourt Brace Jovanovich, 1984, p. 142.
3. Roe, Betty D., Barbara D. Stoodt, and Paul C. Burns. *Secondary School Reading Instruction, the Content Areas.* Boston, Houghton Mifflin, 1987, p. 4.
4. Leu, Donald J. and Charles K. Kinzer. *Effective Reading Instruction in the Elementary Grades.* Columbus, Charles E. Merrill, 1987, p. 166.
5. Heilman, Arthur W., Timothy R. Blair, and William H. Rupley. *Principles and Practices of Teaching Reading* (Sixth Edition). Columbus, Charles E. Merrill, 1986, p. 246.
6. Early, *Reading to Learn,* p. 353.
7. Roe, Stoodt, and Burns, *Secondary School Reading,* p. 68.

8. Zintz, Miles V. and Zelda R. Maggart. *The Reading Process, The Teacher and The Learner* (Fourth Edition). Dubuque, Wm. C. Brown, 1984, p. 236.
9. Pearce, Daniel L., "Guidelines for the Use and Evaluation of Writing in Content Classrooms." *Journal of Reading,* Vol. 27, No. 3 (December, 1983), p. 213.

Chapter IV

BUILDING EFFECTIVE COMPREHENSION SKILLS IN EVERY SECONDARY CLASS

The end product of the reading act is that of comprehension or meaning derived from the printed symbols. By the time students reach the secondary level, they are obligated to read materials of a more complex nature that involve technical vocabulary and integrated concepts. Subject area teachers are often the most qualified school faculty to help students with their comprehension-needs instruction. These instructors are acquainted with the nature of the reading material and style of writing as well as other facets of the printed matter assignments required. Faculty members need only to make minor instructional changes to help students improve their comprehension skill levels.[1]

The entire area of comprehension is composed of a multitude of skills that can be grouped into three major levels: literal, interpretive, and critical. The major goal of reading is to receive the message or communication which the writer desires to extend to the reader. If comprehension competencies are to be developed, a number of factors and/or conditions must be present. These include a proper background of understanding on the part of the student, with appropriate questioning strategies promoted by the teacher. A learner's success in any school environment is highly correlated with his/her ability to comprehend both the printed text materials and the data delivered via lectures by the secondary teacher. Many of the critical and creative reading skill competencies are refined at the high school level. To provide useful help for the secondary teacher in supplying appropriate instruction in this important area, the following topics are explored in this chapter: principles of efficient comprehension instruction, factors affecting comprehension ability, levels of comprehension, effective methods for improving comprehension skills, and techniques for evaluating comprehension competency.

PRINCIPLES OF EFFICIENT
COMPREHENSION INSTRUCTION

Every content teacher is responsible for promoting comprehension skill abilities in his/her subject area and should think of the total reading instructional skills program as being an integrated process rather than a single subject. The following are some of the major aspects to remember in planning learning activities that are designed to improve comprehension abilities.

1. **Comprehension requires the application of skills that have been learned previously.** Rapid word recognition and a large store of vocabulary and concepts will enable students to read quickly and understand what they have just studied.[2] Accordingly, appropriate evaluation must be made of each student's *present* reading abilities to determine if further instruction and remedial training are required before extensive assignments involving comprehension are given. A careful analysis should be made of the various components of the reading section of the latest achievement test. For example, the following questions may be used as a guide for the evaluation.

   a. Is this student below grade level achievement in overall vocabulary?
   b. Does the factor analysis indicate a decided weakness in certain comprehension skill strands (i.e. reading for details)?
   c. Compared with other students at this grade level, is there need to give the learner further training in improving reading rate?
   d. What is the overall relationship between scores received on the reading section and other segments of the examination?

2. **The nature of the questions and purposes established by the secondary content teacher has a significant correlation with the level of comprehension or meaning attained.** One of the basic causes of inadequate comprehension is lack of purpose for reading. As Nessel[3] points out, the use of prior knowledge and prediction is clearly of great value in helping students set purposes for reading while using their own experiences as a basis for comprehending the text. A global assignment that has a general direction lacks the degree of specificity which allows the learner to remember intended data and/or concepts. If, in a history class, the instructor merely asks the students "to read Chapter 4 and we will talk about it," the learners have little direction about *what* is to be remembered. A better

assignment would be: (a) Find the three reasons why President Johnson was nearly impeached; and (b) Locate the names of the three senators who led the drive for impeachment. This type of questioning outlines the specific *kinds* of information that should be remembered.

In the case of a literature class, the instructor may give specific directions calling for the simple retelling of a story. Kalmbach[4] believes that recall forces the reader to attend to what is taken away from reading. Communicating a point in a retelling forces the reader to attend to the experience of reading, since perception of a point will depend both on the text and the experiences, expectations, and prejudices that the reader brings to the act of reading.

The importance of asking the right kinds of questions serves a variety of purposes. At their best, questions trigger inquiry and application and transform students from information seekers to information users. It is important to ask the right kinds of questions. Instructors should avoid the impression that there is only *one* right answer or to use the activity as an interrogation session to merely find if the students have "read the text."[5]

Questions or purposes for reading any kind of chapter or unit material may be arranged in a structured outline in which prepared assignments are made that call for the recall of specific information. For example, a science teacher may wish to prepare three columns on a lesson sheet which require certain kinds of data. In column one, this question may be printed: "What four chemicals are required for performing the experiment dealing with carbon dioxide?" In column two the learners are directed to list four profitable uses of carbon dioxide gas. The third column may be used for the listing of five gases that have similar properties as carbon dioxide.

3. **The structured overview may be utilized as an important teaching device for helping students of all ability levels to comprehend desired concepts at a maximum rate.** With this technique the teacher and/or students select important concepts and vocabulary and arrange them in a graphic design for introduction and discussion before reading.[6] There are numerous kinds of structured overviews; however, it is highly recommended that secondary students be given an active part in the building of the outline. They may, for example, wish to help arrange a list of vocabulary terms with connecting lines in order to understand the proper concepts that may exist among and between certain words. For example, a structured

overview of a science unit on the study of planet life may look similar to the following.

All living things

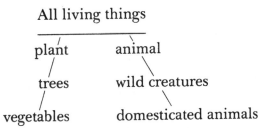

The list of words selected can be review words as well as words which are about to be introduced in the new unit. The instructor should explain to the class why the words are arranged in the manner demonstrated. The reasons for the arrangement should be explained.

A related procedure that may be used is to list the words and their respective meanings. The words could be placed on cards, and small groups of students can experiment placing the cards in various designs to simulate a semantic mapping strategy. This type of structured overview transfers the responsibility for prediction from the teacher to the students. Secondary instructors should be sure that the relationships involved are fairly simple and obvious so the learners will not be thwarted in their efforts.[7]

In summary, the structured overview represents an important strategy for giving students an advance knowledge of the facts, concepts, and ideas that are to be presented in a body of assigned printed matter.

4. **The material that is to be read and comprehended should be at the approximate instructional reading level of the students.** Many reading authorities agree that this is the level represented by a particular textbook where the student can pronounce 95 to 97 percent of the words correctly while reading orally and demonstrate a score of 75 to 89 percent on a teacher-prepared silent-reading comprehension examination involving the material. A readability formula can be used to gain an *estimation* of the reading difficulty of a given book. Formulas that may be used with secondary level books include the SMOG, FRY and DALE–CHALL. Edward Fry[8] notes that readability formulas have been in existence for at least 60 years, and over a thousand articles have been published about the technique. They are not only being used by teachers to match the learner's reading ability to the difficulty level of class texts, but many business authorities, government agents, and publishers are employing them to help insure the appropriate readability levels of such items as

insurance policies, directions for using a product, and the appropriate level of difficulty of certain textbooks and workbooks.

Some companies have now produced software for use with various microcomputers such as those by Apple and Radio Shack. By typing in a designated body of material from a desired source, the printer delivers a final copy which indicates data regarding the readability level of the material according to several different formulas. (One such piece of software is called *Readability Calculations* and is produced by Micro Power and Light Company, 12820 Hillcrest Road, Suite 219, Dallas, Texas 75230.)

5. **If adequate comprehension is to be insured, consideration should be given to spending sufficient time for building a background of experience and appreciation for the topics about to be read.** Secondary teachers can gain an impression of the general level of interest and experience of their students through the use of both oral and written questions. For the more difficult topics, the instructor needs to make the decision to either skip these topics completely or plan to spend a considerable amount of time in building a background of concepts for the topic. Many students who have experienced deprivations of an educational and/or cultural nature may find the assigned lessons to be much too difficult to understand and thus will no doubt exhibit insufficient levels of literal, interpretive, and critical comprehension. These learners may need exposure to supplementary study materials, audiovisual presentations, and additional discussions on the part of the instructor.

6. **If an effective level of comprehension is to be achieved, students need to match their speed of reading to their reading purpose and the readability level of the text material.** One of the major reasons for ineffective comprehension of printed matter at the secondary level is the use of an inappropriate reading rate for the purpose that the reader has in mind. In recent years much attention has been drawn to commercial and private reading clinics which advertise that one can "double reading speed without loss of comprehension." Becker[9] notes, on the contrary, that it is doubtful that speed reading enhances comprehension and analytical thinking skills on the assumption that people read too slow to think naturally. He contends that even memory experts relate episodes of how fickle and arbitrary the mind and memory are, and of the emotional aspects of information storage, not to mention the limitations of the brain's ability to deal with various amounts and kinds of information.

The major aspect for students to remember is to match reading speed with

the types and kinds of comprehension or communication desired. In a social studies class when students are expected to read large amounts of material and remember dozens of facts and concepts, the instructor should remind them to read at a slow, deliberate speed of perhaps 100 words or less per minute. If main ideas is the goal, a moderate rate of 400 words may be useful; whereas, the quick recognition of a single word or phrase may be obtained by skimming or scanning at 1,000 to 2,000 words a minute.

7. **Careful attention should be given to the selection and use of instructional materials for building comprehension in light of each student's favored learning modality and cultural background.** Those students who learn best through the visual modality need to have a large number of books and articles that have a significant number of pictures, drawings, diagrams, and other types of illustrative material. Films, filmstrips, and computer lessons with many graphics may also be helpful. Those that prefer auditory modes may comprehend better through the use of tapes and lectures which emphasize the major aspects of a printed text.

With respect to culture, Berliner[10] is of the belief that teachers have no choice but to inquire into each learner's unique culture and learning history to determine what instructional materials might best be used and to determine when a student's cultural and life experiences are compatible or potentially incompatible with instruction. To do less is to build emotional blocks to communication in an already complicated instructional situation. In all cases we learn that culture and subculture membership influence how and what we learn.

8. **When emphasizing the teaching of comprehension, emphasis should be given to instructional procedures that are compatible for those learners who may be right-brained.** The processing of information by the brain is naturally an important element in building important concepts after a subject reads a body of print material. The left cerebral hemisphere tends to be the focus for linear-sequential thinking, reading, writing, and the ordering of language processes, while the right side deals more with the processing of information simultaneously and intuitively.[11] Many disabled readers at the secondary level are prone to have a preference for right-brain functioning, and thus content teachers should be aware of certain strategies that may materially help these students improve overall comprehension ability.

To assist the student who may be right-brained, the following teaching principles may be emphasized:

a. Lessons and classroom activities that require ordered listening may be useful. A partial reading of a story by the teacher may take place. After reaching a crucial stage in the selection, students are asked to write their interpretation of how the story might end. Leading the class to predict the ending and become emotionally involved in the selection is highly important.

b. Semantic mapping helps the right-brained learner to integrate the various segments of a story or a discussion section regarding a social studies or science topic. The teacher could perhaps place four large circles on a chart or a transparency and indicate the major aspects of the topic or selection. Students should be invited to place diagonal lines from each segment and place ideas, facts, and concepts that relate to the basic story segments in circles at the end of the lines. This activity gives the right-brained learner a chance to engage in meaningful divergent thinking and the building of knowledge relating to spatial relationships.

9. If a significant group of students display problems with comprehension, a special effort should be made to use high interest/low vocabulary materials to supplement the regular text sources. These types of print media present a minimum of problems since they emphasize topics and subjects that demand a very limited schemata or background of understanding for the reading assignment. Many of the books of this nature present statements of both a literal and interpretive nature that can be easily assimilated by most readers, including those who read at a below grade level efficiency. Even more able students find the selections interesting since they can be read in a limited amount of time.

10. Five sequential steps should be followed for teaching other major reading comprehension skills in all content areas. The introduction and teaching the meaning of words and various concepts can be accomplished successfully if the following steps are undertaken in every class session where print media is required reading.

I. Background Stage

At the beginning of the lesson the secondary instructor needs to call attention to all of the following aspects:

a. Survey of the major and minor topics presented in order to gain an idea of the facts and concepts that are outlined. Special attention should be given to the names of both major and minor headings as well as the words, phrases, and sentences that are either/and italicized and printed in bold type.

b. Inquiry sessions with students to determine the depth and latitude of information already known about the topic to be read.

c. Motivation discussion with students to generate interest in the topic and relate how the coming assignment is correlated with previous and future lessons in the subject curriculum.

II. Purposes Stage

As noted in the next section, a leading factor involved in the successful comprehension of the silent reading of any body of print material is that of having a *reason or purpose for reading*. Questions to guide the silent reading should be formulated *before* the silent reading is undertaken. The number and types of questions posed for the learners will depend on their age and maturity levels; however, most secondary students should be able to assimilate at least four to six major questions that may be given, for example, over a segment of 12–15 pages of a social studies or science text. The questions should be both subjective and objective in nature and be representative of all three levels of comprehension: *literal, interpretative,* and *critical.* For example, if the American history class is assigned to read the chapter, "The American Revolution," the following questions may be appropriate:

Literal: The hired troops in the British army were called by what name?

Interpretive: Look at the five paragraphs on Pages 80–81 regarding the Battle of Yorktown. What was the most important main idea that can be learned from this section?

Critical: Is the following statement a fact or opinion? The British troops were commonly called "redcoats."

III. Silent Reading Activity

After questions and purposes have been established, students should be directed to those text materials that contain the data and information needed to fulfill reading purposes. A variety of materials should be available on different levels of reading difficulty to accommodate those learners who possess below average, average, and above average reading abilities.

IV. Discussion Activity

The purposes or questions established for the silent reading should serve as the basis for a meaningful discussion after the silent reading has taken place. Reinforcement or remedial instruction may be needed for individual students who have difficulty finding sufficient answers for the reading purposes.

V. Culminating Level

The results of studies dealing with learning theory suggest that appropriate correlations should be made between and among the topics studied in the past and those currently being explored. Better comprehension results when the students are able to see both primary and secondary relationships that exist among the different study segments.

FACTORS AFFECTING COMPREHENSION ABILITY

Unfortunately, large numbers of students in any content class have difficulties of various kinds that prevent them from performing everyday comprehension tasks such as reading for details or selecting the main idea. Generally speaking, one cannot point to a *single* cause for reading comprehension deficiency such as lack of phonics ability or some physical disability. Students who appear to be average or above average in overall academic ability and demonstrate inadequate comprehension skill development should be assessed through the use of both formal and informal evaluation instruments to help pinpoint the probable causes of the difficulty. A brief discussion of some possible reasons for inappropriate comprehension development is included in this section.

1. **Unsatisfactory Fundamental Word-Attack Skill Proficiency.** Since reading skill development should be sequential in most respects, comprehension requires the application of many skills that have been learned already. Rapid word recognition and a large store of vocabulary will enable students to read quickly with good understanding. The greater the background of information the reader has and applies to what is being read, the better the level of comprehension.[12] Those students who are seriously deficient in comprehension skills should be evaluated by various procedures to assess the degree of word-attack proficiency. Listening carefully to students as they read orally may lend valuable data

regarding knowledge of phonic skills, structural analysis, and ability to utilize context clues.

2. Presence of Emotional Problems. In order to comprehend important details and main ideas while reading silently, complete attention to the task of reading is required. Estimates of the significance of emotional factors in the causation of reading disabilities vary widely. Most students with reading difficulties show signs of emotional maladjustment which may be mild or severe. The percentage of maladjustment reported by a particular investigator varies with the standards used, as well as the student population studied.[13]

Today's adolescents may be involved in home environments where physical and/or emotional abuse may be present. Many individuals have emotional problems so severe that suicidal tendencies may develop. In fact, according to many current research studies, suicide is thought to be the second leading cause of death among young people in the United States. Referral of a student to a school counselor or other professional for therapy and ongoing counseling may be necessary before significant improvement can take place in the area of reading skills in general and comprehension ability in particular.

3. Lack of Purpose for Reading. One of the leading causes of ineffective comprehension is lack of purpose for reading. In far too many instances a teacher may say casually, "Read Chapter 10 for tomorrow and we will discuss it." This particular assignment may contain numerous detailed paragraphs of material that contain dozens of facts, figures, and difficult concepts and have several subheadings with a variety of topics introduced. In this situation, the learner is not sure if he or she is to read to remember specific details, certain main ideas, or a single generalization. Since it is entirely possible for the teacher and student to have very divergent goals, the young person will probably study and remember incorrect information and be unprepared for a discussion or test over the material.

Shepherd[14] notes that many students read an assignment because they are told to do so. When questioned, these students have at best only a fuzzy idea of what they are to learn except "the information in this chapter or on these pages."

When a reading assignment is given, precise questions or purposes must be given that involve all three levels of inquiry: literal, interpretive, and critical. This type of questioning was discussed earlier in this chapter.

4. Difficulty with Understanding Vocabulary of the Assigned Material. Words are the basic units of meaning in a language. It seems self-evident, therefore, that understanding a message which is made up of words should require some degree of familiarity with those words.[15] To discover if the difficulty of the reading material matches the instructional reading level of the learner, a vocabulary pretest can be administered. (If the student receives a score of less than 80 percent correct, the teacher may want to replace the assigned books with less difficult passages.) The following may be sample items from such a test.

1. *Delete* means to (a) enlarge something, (b) make smaller, (c) leave out.
2. *Luminary* refers to a (a) light-giving body, (b) high government official, (c) police officer.

5. Inappropriate Background of Experience. The act of reading requires much more than the mere pronunciation of words. Meaning must be associated with the words if the correct message is to be received by the reader. If there is evidence that students lack a sufficient understanding of the words in a passage or story, the teacher is obliged to undertake a variety of strategies to help build a bridge of understanding for these learners. Teaching activities may include the use of films, bulletin boards, experiments, and appropriate software for use in the class computer. Directed discussions using models and charts may be helpful for promoting understanding. The results of a vocabulary pretest as described in the previous section may dictate the amount of background teaching that may be necessary.

6. Physical Difficulties. The ability to derive meaning from a word, sentence, or paragraph is a very complex operation and requires the reader to perceive symbols correctly and interpret what they mean in light of his/her background of experience. The status of one's hearing and vision has a significant correlation with the amount and degree of comprehension that may be realized. Any summary of the research in the area of vision, hearing, and reading could safely conclude that in most cases reading achievement is not directly related to vision and hearing, but in some cases specific defects of vision and hearing may be contributing factors to reading disability.[16]

Adolescents may possess significant health problems that may detract considerably from one's ability to comprehend print materials. These include the use of legal and illegal drugs, brain damage, neurological difficulties, and glandular disturbances. Those students who come from impoverished home backgrounds may be malnourished, overtired, or possess general health problems. Secondary teachers should refer those students with suspected physical difficulties to the school nurse and/or physician for diagnosis and proper treatment of the problems. Unless this course of action is followed, there is little likelihood that overall comprehension will improve.

7. **Inability to Follow Author's Organization of Material.** Each author of a content textbook usually constructs a framework or outline of the basic ideas, topics, and data to be presented. The table of contents reveals the names of the chapter titles and subtitles. Each chapter has a specific name, and subtopics are often indented and italicized and/or printed in heavy black type. Some books have end-of-chapter summaries and a list of questions or other types of activities for the reader to complete. If a given group of students are to be successful in comprehending the overall body of information, it is imperative that they be given direct instruction by each teacher at the *beginning* of the semester. The logical presentation of the material can be explained and study hints given to help them separate very important to less vital information. If necessary, instruction can be provided relative to such aspects as the meaning and use of topic sentences, the SQ3R reading-study formula, and the correct methods to utilize for outlining chapter material.

8. **Absence of Skills for Separating Literal and Critical Comprehension Components.** Many adolescent readers (as well as older persons) are prone to accept as *the truth* all and every statement they read. All too often students are heard to say, "I read it in the paper, so it must be true!" To help alleviate undue allegiance to what is read or heard, careful attention should be given to a number of questions. Questions that might be asked relative to this area may include:

   a. **Do you see any propaganda techniques such as "card-stacking," "name-calling," and "identification with prestige?"**
   b. **What evidence does the author give for making such a statement?**
   c. **Is statement number 4 a figure of speech or should we believe exactly what it says?**

If class members have difficulty in dealing with appropriate response to these questions, the teacher needs to give direct instruction to the following aspects: kinds of figurative expressions (metaphors, similes, etc); the types of propaganda techniques with appropriate examples; and methods of detecting the presence (or lack of) of evidence for a given conclusion. Propaganda techniques can be taught by showing examples of such items in the editorial and advertising sections of the local newspaper. Figurative language can be understood more clearly by asking students to circle or underline examples of figurative language which are included in a selection compiled by the instructor or a commercial publisher.

9. **Insufficient Level of General Intelligence.** For some students the ability to comprehend printed matter of both literal and critical types is somewhat restricted because of a limited level of overall intelligence. The results of many research studies appear to show that there is a significant positive relationship between intelligence and comprehension ability, especially at the secondary and adult levels. This premise is even more reliable if the intelligence quotient has been obtained by a trained examiner using the *Wechsler* or *Binet* instrument.

Hill[17] is of the belief that the relationship between intelligence test scores and reading test scores remains the highest obtained between any single human characteristic and reading performance. The IQ, as an index of relative level of brightness, merits serious consideration in the analysis of reading success. Reading and intelligence are positively correlated variables of human behavior.

The results of some earlier studies suggest that overall general intelligence is more closely parallel to silent reading comprehension in the upper grades and secondary levels than at the primary level. A student's degree of intellectual ability appears to become a more significant factor as the abstractness and semantic structure of print media increases.

All of the previous observations suggest that secondary teachers who encounter students with severely deficient comprehension should be recommended for further intelligence testing. If a below average score is obtained, a student's potential for building a high level of comprehension skill proficiency may be limited.

10. **Inability to Interpret Specialized Features of Text Material.** Many kinds of content textbooks contain such aspects as maps, tables, graphs, diagrams, and complex charts. Each feature is designed to place a large number of facts, concepts, and implications in a limited amount of space. The authors of these materials expect that the typical secondary student has learned the meaning and use of these features during the elementary and middle school years. The fact is, a relatively high percentage of

adolescents have not been taught the meaning and use of these special aspects and either cannot or do not use them.

Since these are valuable text components for relaying different kinds of cognitive material, the lack of use and understanding of these items creates a serious void for the student who has serious need of comprehending information and data for use in taking tests, writing papers, and making an oral class presentation. For these students, the secondary content teacher is obligated to establish special lessons, during which time a detailed explanation is made of certain features. For example, a graph may be shown indicating the rise in population in the United States from the period of 1900 to 1980. To help determine if each student understands the data, the following questions may be asked:

- a. **During what year did the population rise the most?**
- b. **How much gain in population took place between 1930 and 1940?**
- c. **The graph indicates a decline in population during three separate years. What were these years?**

LEVELS OF COMPREHENSION

All information relating to facts and concepts can be placed in three or four levels of understanding. Many teachers are prone to ask oral and written questions that deal only with a large number of minute facts and figures which constitute literal data. Secondary teachers need to challenge students with all levels of questions to keep them thinking, understanding cause and effect, and thinking beyond the convergent levels of right and wrong. Teachers can easily identify three levels of understanding: the literal, the interpretive, and the applied or evaluative one. Each builds on the previous level.[18]

LITERAL COMPREHENSION. This is the lowest level of understanding and may be divided into two divisions: *reproduction*, which merely requires that the reader repeat the writer's words while responding to a question, while *translation*, the higher level of literal comprehension, requires the reader to translate or paraphrase the printed information. Neither level demands much actual thinking or analysis on the part of the reader.[19]

Many older students have the mistaken notion that *every* sentence is important in a textbook and feel that all information must be learned in a literal manner. They typically use a felt-tip marker and proceed to shade the vast majority of the sentences on a given page. The learner is driven to utter distraction since they find they cannot discriminate between the more important and less valuable facts and concepts that are printed. If this situation is discovered by the content teacher, he or she should provide directed instruction relative to the four levels of comprehension. He or she should emphasize that while the remembering of literal facts is important, skill must be gained in dealing with data representing the other three levels as well.

INTERPRETIVE COMPREHENSION. Knowing what the author says is necessary but not sufficient in constructing meaning from print. Good readers search for conceptual complexity in material. They are capable of "reading between the lines" and focus not only on what the authors say but also on what the authors mean by what they say.[20] The interpretive or inference level consists of a number of skill components such as the following.

a. **Selecting** the single *main idea* of a body of information such as a paragraph or chapter.
b. **Discovering** the sequence of events that are described in a story, play or informative chapter and may be found in a history text.
c. **Drawing** conclusions that are logical products of a descriptive or informative article that may be found in a science, social studies, or literature text.
d. **Inferring** cause-and-effect relationships when those relationships and correlations are not directly stated.
e. **Predicting** outcomes of both fictional and informational types of materials.
f. **Generating** comparisons of such aspects as likenesses and differences in characters, times, and places.
g. **Understanding** the precise meaning of various kinds of figurative language such as similes and metaphors.

CRITICAL COMPREHENSION. At this level adolescent readers are to be actively involved in determining the truthfulness or authenticity of a statement based on their background of experience and ability to make relevant judgments about the information contained in the articles and books that are required reading. At this stage they should develop a discerning attitude that not all statements in a newspaper or book are necessarily true. Accordingly, they should develop skill in making educated judgments about whether:

a. A statement is a fact or an opinion.
b. A story is reality or fantasy.
c. The writer uses one or more propaganda techniques to promote certain ideas.
d. The material has any basic worth when compared with other articles on the same subject.
e. The text material has accuracy and truthfulness in terms of some criteria which the reader has formulated based on his/her previous experience.

One of the most important critical reading skills is that of the identification of various commonly used propaganda techniques. Readers should be given appropriate instruction to allow them to identify examples of such techniques as:

Name-calling. (He is a *self-centered conservative* on most political matters.)

Glittering generalities. (Everuse shoes are the standard for the discriminating buyer.)

Plain-folks device. (Your good neighbor, Mr. Brown, plans to vote for John Hopewell for governor.)

Testimonials. (Eight out of ten teachers, according to a recent survey, prefer Everdry chalk to all other brands.)

Identification with prestige. (Troy Proger, king of all cowboys, uses Jones Underslung Saddles on all of his horses.)

Bandwagon effect. (The Wilson poll shows that 82 percent of all registered voters prefer William Jensen for mayor.)

Card-stacking. (Based on the number of actual hours taught, teachers compose one of the highest paid professions now in existence.)

EFFECTIVE METHODS FOR IMPROVING COMPREHENSION SKILLS

As noted in the previous paragraphs, there are a variety of skills that should be stressed at all three levels of comprehension. The following suggestions may be used in a number of situations and can be applied in one or more content areas with relative ease and a high degree of success. The ideas are listed in no particular order of priority or importance and apply generally to the literal and interpretive levels.

1. **The assessment of overall comprehension and vocabulary ability can be accomplished through the use of a cloze procedure instrument.** The instrument can be constructed by using regular class text material that contains about 2 to 5 pages. The following steps should be followed:

   a. Type the first sentence *exactly* as it appears in the material.
   b. Starting with the second sentence, leave every fifth word blank until a sum total of 50 omissions have been accumulated.
   c. Ask students to read the exercise carefully and write the most appropriate word they can think of on each of the blanks.
   d. Check each paper utilizing the words from the *original* source as the key for grading. Do not accept synonyms or substitutions. **Those students who have grade level competency in comprehension should score in the 18–25 correct range.** Those who score less than 18 are below grade level and those who score above 26 are above grade level in competency.

2. **One important procedure for gaining practice and skill in the interpretive skills is that of placing significant events in their proper order.** After studying a body of historical or scientific material, list in scrambled fashion a number of such facts. Ask students to place them in the correct chronological order.

3. **Use the local newspaper as an important teaching material for giving students practice in the identification of propaganda techniques.** Using a structured discussion, explain to students the meaning and nature of the more common propaganda techniques that were noted in an earlier part of this chapter. Supply each student with a copy of the local newspaper. Encourage them to study carefully various news stories, editorials, and advertisements to find examples of such techniques. The class can be divided into small groups, with each group to concentrate on just one technique (e.g. identification with prestige). After a designated period of time, a classwide discussion can be conducted regarding the number and kind of different examples found.

A related creative assignment may involve the placement of a familiar object, such as an overhead projector, on a table and inviting students to create a newspaper advertisement promoting the item. Encourage them to use a maximum number of propaganda techniques as part of their project.

4. **Brainstorming is a viable approach for both the analysis and building of an appropriate schemata in a particular area of study.** Teachers can brainstorm with an individual, small group, or an entire class.[21] The instruc-

tor should write the name of a chapter or unit topic on the chalkboard and students are asked to say the first words that come to their mind. After all of the words have been written, the teacher and students should decide if all words listed are relevant.

5. **To gain competency in selecting the main idea of a selection, supply copies of a feature news article from the local newspaper to all class members and ask them to construct a logical headline for the article.** An alternative plan may be that of providing a sample list of headline titles and asking students to select the *one* title that most closely correlates with the content of the news article. With either activity, show the students the headline used by the newspaper for comparison with the titles they chose.

6. **A well-structured listening activity can serve to amplify the importance of remembering important details.** The instructor should read four of five paragraphs aloud from a related class text or source book and ask students to write as many separate details as they can remember. They should not be permitted to record notes during the time the material is read aloud. An alternate activity could consist of the students responding to a true-false examination. They should mark *true* (+) for all statements or facts actually mentioned during the reading and *false* (o) for those not read.

7. **Teaching the sequence of events is an important comprehension skill to refine in such areas as social studies and science.** Constructing *time lines* in social studies, for example, is an effective tool for helping students recall when certain events took place. Designated learners can be assigned to record significant pieces of information such as the names of presidents, dates of wars and significant battles, and various economic events such as the Great Depression. The long chart can be placed at the side or front of the room, with vertical lines painted with various colors to designate the events. Volunteers can be invited to illustrate various events and activities associated with each major segment of the chart.

Another related strategy is the completion of a *flowchart.* Several boxes may be constructed in sequential order that relates to the regular steps which must be followed to complete an experiment, for example. The following is a sample of such a flowchart.

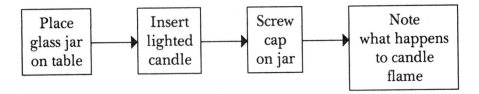

8. **The ability to follow directions is one of the most important of all literal comprehension skills to develop.** The following are two useful activities that may be utilized with secondary students.

   a. Provide each student with a copy of a job application form and ask them to complete the form according to the printed directions. Evaluate each section of the form and explain for students the area or areas where they have made possible errors.
   b. Ask students to participate in an exercise that is designed to emphasize the importance of following directions in an *exact manner.* At the top of the sheet print the following statement: **Read all of the directions for the exercise** *before* **attempting to supply any of the answers. The first statement may read: Write your teacher's name on the blank that follows.** The second, third and fourth statements may have similar requests. At the end of the exercise write the following directions: **Do not complete the answers for any of the previous statements. Hand in your paper to your teacher without delay.** The impact should be dramatic and pointed.

9. **All secondary students should develop the ability to read maps, graphs, and charts and draw special facts and main ideas that may be a part of the figures.**

   a. With regard to a map, the learners should gain the facility to pronounce and define numerous words and phrases that are a unique part of any given map. For example, words and phrases such as the following may be a part of vocabulary enlargement: **longitude, latitude, peninsula, isthmus, international date line, tropical belt, and equator.**

   Thorough instruction must be given relative to the meaning and importance of various symbols on the map. Following this instruction, numerous questions and queries may be composed such as the following:

   1. In what European country can be found the highest mountains? _____
   2. Name the largest city in the country of Portugal. _____
   3. It is approximately ____ miles from Paris to Frankfort.
   4. Name two countries which lie south of the equator. _____
   5. True or False. The population of London is greater than that of Zurich. _____

   b. The meaning and importance of bar graphs should be undertaken. Emphasize that, in addition, there are pictorial, line, and circle graphs. Select a bar graph on a given page of the class text for careful study. Point out various features of the chart and show how certain facts and concepts can be derived from it. To see if the students understand the meaning of the various features of the chart, provide the students with a list of fact-opinion statements relating to the information on the chart. The following are sample items that may be utilized from a chart showing the growth of the national debt of the United States Government.

_____ The national debt was twice as large in 1960 as it was in 1930.
_____ The most significant five-year gain in the debt occurred during the period from 1980–1985.
_____ The debt in 1980 was over $1 trillion.
_____ The debt grew at a slower rate from 1940 to 1950 than it did from 1970–1980.

Another class project may be undertaken by supplying class members with a body of data relating to some phases of the school information fact sheet. These data may include enrollment of students in each grade, home districts of students, and related information. With the data before them, class members may construct a bar or circle graph that illustrates the information available.

10. One of the major content reading skills that should be developed by all secondary students is that of summarizing a body of information which has been read recently. There are a number of competencies necessary if one is to be efficient in summarizing large segments of printed matter. The student must understand the correlations and relationships between and among the specific facts and main ideas that are presented. They must understand how to locate the topic sentence and its importance to all preceding sentences. By remembering the main ideas of a selection, a *good* reader should have the ability to condense and organize the statements into a meaningful summary of the assigned material.

TECHNIQUES FOR EVALUATING COMPREHENSION COMPETENCY

In order to build an effective set of strategies for strengthening comprehension skills, instructors must establish a systematic program of evaluation procedures for use with students on both a group and individual basis. For a system of evaluation in the area of comprehension to be effective and useful, several conditions must be present in the school and classroom environment. They are: (1) definitive objectives for constructing comprehension and related skills; (2) faculty members who are devoted to a program of both formal and informal evaluation; (3) a commitment to approaching reading skills instruction from a process rather than a strict subject point of view; and (4) the overall knowledge of the strengths and limitations of various evaluation techniques.

Secondary instructors must always think of comprehension evaluation in the broadest sense and should encompass a variety of features, including test data derived from formal achievement tests (such as the *Nelson-Denny*); results of student achievement when responding to various comprehension level questions composed by the teacher; and information derived about a particular student's attitude toward comprehension through observation as well as verbal and non-verbal cues.

When using both formal and informal measures to evaluate a secondary student's level of comprehension skill ability, several important guidelines or principles should be remembered.

1. **Evaluation of comprehension abilities should be thought of as a continuous as well as a periodic endeavor.** Daily assessments should be made through the study of the oral and written responses of students that relate to different types of comprehension questions posed by the secondary teacher. Daily contact with each student which involves assessment of comprehension skills will help to provide data that will help the secondary teacher prepare lessons that are individualized and pinpointed to meet a special instructional need. Following this principle allows the instructor to seize the most teachable moment or time for appropriate comprehension skills instruction.

2. **Secondary teachers need to keep in mind that the major purpose for evaluating comprehension abilities is to gain meaningful data for improving instruction.** An analysis of a composite of scores should reveal if individual or collective groups of students are strong or limited in the important skill strands of reading for details, gaining main ideas, and summarizing significant paragraphs. Instructors must remember that a careful analysis of data may reveal the clear conclusion that an alteration is necessary in the current teaching strategies. Perhaps the focus of the course objectives need changing along with the types of teaching materials utilized.

3. **The purpose of the administration of evaluative instruments should be explained to the students.** They should understand that the major thrust of the activities is that of altering the teaching program to meet their *personal* needs. Unfortunately, too many adolescents believe that the sole purpose of testing is that of providing a basis for constructing a grade. If

students understand that the total evaluation program is designed to strengthen their present comprehension levels, they will be prone to exhibit their best efforts when completing tests and class exercises.

The most common means of evaluating comprehension ability is through the use of commercial reading tests. The following is a list of widely used achievement tests that contain components dealing with current comprehension skill ability.

Standardized Tests

California Reading Tests (CTB, McGraw-Hill) levels 14–19 measure both vocabulary and comprehension. The comprehension section yields valuable information relating to literal, interpretive, and critical reading.

Degrees of Reading Power Tests (College Board) is a newer test that yields valuable data which helps teachers match the reading skill level of the student with the readability level of the texts they are using. The secondary student's skill in the various comprehension levels has a significant relationship to the final score achieved on the instrument.

Gates-MacGinitie Reading Tests (Riverside) measure several factors, including total comprehension.

Iowa Tests of Educational Development (Science Research Associates) contain a number of subtests that result in a reading score which indicates a student's level of comprehension skill ability in a number of content areas.

Metropolitan Achievement Test (Harcourt Brace Jovanovich) provides for several levels of testing, including an advanced level that measures comprehension skills, vocabulary, and skimming and scanning.

Nelson-Denny Reading Test (Riverside) is a popular achievement instrument for secondary students and measures ability in the areas of vocabulary, comprehension, and reading rate.

S.R.A. Survey of Basic Skills (Science Research Associates) is a battery of materials that are suitable for secondary students and measure a variety of reading skill components, including vocabulary and comprehension.

Standard Achievement Tests (Harcourt Brace Jovanovich) contain a number of segments, including the Advanced Battery for Grades 1–9, and evaluate vocabulary and comprehension as well as other skill segments.

Informal Techniques

The estimate of a student's level of comprehension ability should be judged by utilizing data from a number of sources. While the scores from the previously named achievement tests are helpful in this regard, teachers must utilize other means of estimating the range and general levels of reading abilities in their classes. Teachers must continue to adjust their strategies throughout the year as they gather evidence of strengths and weaknesses from students' daily performances.[22] The informal techniques that are described in this section are excellent strategies to employ since they relate to the actual materials and objectives.

I. The Cloze Test

The directions for constructing this instrument were given in an earlier part of this chapter. The responses supplied by students for the omitted words can lend much help to secondary teachers in analyzing the strengths and limitations of individual students with regard to all four of the comprehension levels. The *schemata* or background of understanding can be judged by studying the kinds of words. written by learners. To gain reliable data regarding the suitability of a given text for any individual student requires the administration of five to seven cloze tests from the text, since topics and kinds of material differ considerably from one section to another. The *average* score derived from the several tests should be used for assessing overall readability level and comprehension ability. As noted earlier, a score in the range of 18–25 on a 50-blank test suggests that the material in the text is at the approximate reading level of the learner.

II. Written Recall Exercise

One of the most practical means of evaluating comprehension abilities is the use of a simple written recall test. The following directions may be used.

1. Select a passage that encompasses approximately three pages of material from a school-adopted content book. The paragraphs should be considered representative of the total volume and should not have been read previously by the students.

2. Tell the students that they should read the selection, with the goal of trying to remember as many details as possible. They should be told

that there will be a fifteen-minute time limit for reading the exercise and *no* notes may be taken during the exercise. If they finish reading before the time has expired, they are welcome to reread as much of the material as they desire.

3. At the close of fifteen minutes, they should be directed to close their books. A series of duplicated questions should be distributed to them for the recording of their responses. A designated percent of the final grade should be indicated for each of the questions. The questions should be representative of all three comprehension levels. Sample items for each of the levels can be found in an earlier part of this chapter.

4. All papers should be carefully graded and an assessment made according to a standard similar to the following: 75 to 89 percent correct indicates adequate or average comprehension ability for the affected grade level; 90 to 100 percent denotes above average ability; less than 75 percent suggests an unsatisfactory comprehension skill level.

One cannot, of course, assign any absolute qualities to a test of this nature. Accordingly, those who score less than 75 percent should be questioned further using oral-type questions. Certain factors may prove to be restrictive aspects for some learners, and a more reliable means of assessment can be obtained through the use of further oral questioning.

III. *Informal Review of Reading Attitudes*

A student's attitudes toward reading has considerable influence with reference to how he or she succeeds in comprehending everyday reading assignments. The following review may be utilized with secondary students using either of two different methods. *First,* it may be given to class members to complete by writing in their desired responses. They should be informed that their information will be held in strictest confidence and, therefore, they should be frank and truthful with their responses. The material they supply has *no* relationship to their grade in the class. They should be informed that the major reason for the exercise is to provide background data that will help the teacher provide better assignments and overall instruction for them.

Second, the form can be utilized for conducting individual interviews with the teacher or counselor writing the oral responses on the form. An excellent rapport should be established and the students informed that their responses will be regarded as personal and confidential.

<u>Informal Review of Reading Attitudes</u>

Name _____ Grade _____ Date _____

1. Do you describe yourself as an excellent, average, or below average reader? Why have you arrived at this decision?

_____
_____
_____

2. Other than class assignments, how much and what kind of reading do you undertake for your own pleasure?

_____
_____
_____

3. When you are assigned a chapter of material to be read, how do you undertake the reading assignment to help insure that you will remember what you have read?

_____
_____
_____

4. Do you have trouble remembering many of the details you have just read? *If you do,* which of the following items may have caused your difficulty?
_____ Don't understand the topic
_____ No interest in the material
_____ Can't decide what I am supposed to remember
_____ My mind seems to be on other things that happened at home or other places
_____ Seem to study the wrong things
_____ The teacher does not give me enough time to answer the questions.

5. Your teacher would like to help you study better and remember more of what you have read. Use the space below to list any suggestions that your instructor can use to help you with these areas.

SUMMARY

There are numerous important principles to remember when constructing an effective program of comprehension instruction. Some students have difficulty with comprehending because of any one or more of the factors that are discussed in this chapter. All secondary instructors should remember that there are three distinct levels of comprehension, and both written and oral questions should be asked relating to each of these areas. The tested methods for innovative classroom strategies for improving and evaluating comprehension skills can be employed in virtually all content areas. One of the most important principles to remember is that comprehension skill competency should be a high priority by *all* teachers in *all* content areas.

REFERENCES

1. Forgan, Harry W. and Charles T. Mangrum II, *Teaching Content Area Reading Skills* (Second Edition). Columbus, Charles E. Merrill, 1981, p. 150.
2. Zintz, Miles V. and Zelda R. Maggart. *Corrective Reading* (Fifth Edition). Dubuque, Wm. C. Brown, 1986, p. 268.
3. Nessel, Denise, "The New Face of Comprehension Instruction: A Closer Look at Questions." *The Reading Teacher,* V.40, N.7 (March, 1987), p. 604.
4. Kalmbach, James R. "Getting at the Point of Retellings." *Journal of Reading,* V.29, N.4 (January, 1986) p. 333.
5. Vacca, Richard T. and JoAnne Vacca. *Content Area Reading.* Boston, Little, Brown, 1986, pp. 140–141.
6. Clary, Linda M., "Twelve 'Musts' for Improved Reading Comprehension." *Reading Horizons,* V.26, N.2 (January, 1986), p. 102.
7. Early, Margaret. *Reading to Learn in Grades 5 to 12.* New York, Harcourt Brace Jovanovich, 1984, p. 379.
8. Fry, Edward B., "The Varied Uses of Readability Measurement Today." *Journal of Reading,* V.30, N.4 (January, 1987), pp. 338–343.
9. Becker, Brian L.A., "Why Speed Reading Weakens Thinking Processes." *Reading Improvement,* V.24, N.1 (Spring, 1987), p. 6.
10. Berliner, David, "Does Culture Affect Reading Comprehension?" *Instructor,* V.96, No.3 (October, 1986), p. 29.
11. Walker, Barbara J., "Right Brained Strategies for Teaching Comprehension." *Academic Therapy,* V.21, N.2 (November, 1985), pp. 134–135.
12. Zintz, Miles V. and Zelda R. Maggart, *Corrective Reading,* p. 268.
13. Harris, Albert J. and Edward R. Sipay. *How to Increase Reading Ability* (Seventh Edition). New York, Longman, 1980, p. 316.
14. Shepherd, David L. *Comprehensive High School Reading Methods* (Second Edition). Columbus, Charles E. Merrill, 1978, p. 91.
15. Barr, Rebecca and Marilyn Sadow. *Reading Diagnosis for Teachers.* New York, Longman, 1985, p. 69.
16. Karlin, Robert. *Teaching Reading in High School* (Fourth Edition). New York, Harper and Row, 1984, p. 355.

17. Hill, Walter R. *Secondary School Reading: Process, Program, Procedure.* Boston, Allyn and Bacon, 1979, p. 31.
18. Zintz and Maggart, *Corrective Reading,* pp. 280–281.
19. Miller, Wilma. *The First R Elementary Reading Today* (Second Edition). Prospect Heights, Illinois, Waveland Press, 1983, p. 196.
20. Vacca, Richard T. and JoAnne L. Vacca. *Content Area Reading* (Second Edition). Boston, Little, Brown, 1986, p. 147.
21. Roe, Betty D., Barbara D. Stoodt, and Paul C. Burns. *Secondary School Reading Instruction, the Content Areas.* Boston, Houghton Mifflin, 1987, p. 99.
22. Early, Margaret, *Reading to Learn,* p. 147.

Chapter V

ESTABLISHING SIGNIFICANT STUDY SKILLS COMPETENCIES

In order for secondary students to accomplish the goal of comprehending print materials, they need to develop a system of study that will allow them to undertake numerous study skill tasks. Too many secondary teachers assume that their students have learned effective study skills at earlier grade levels and it is not their responsibility to include this type of instruction in their everyday lesson plans. Nearly every student at each of the learning levels needs direct instruction in such important competencies as using library and reference materials, recording class notes, setting a purpose for studying, and taking tests in the most efficient manner.

The major purpose of this chapter is to provide current background information and practical classroom-tested teaching suggestions for helping all secondary students at every ability level to achieve a satisfactory level of competency in the significant study skills areas. Accordingly, the following topics are explored in this chapter: understanding the importance of study skills competencies, constructing adjustable reading rates, using reading-study strategies, and building note-taking techniques.

UNDERSTANDING THE IMPORTANCE OF STUDY SKILLS COMPETENCIES

A casual observation of the study skills habits of many secondary students reveals that many of them have very limited abilities with regard to efficient practices in this area. They may have had a limited degree of direct instruction in such skills as reading with a purpose, using library references, and studying for an examination. The proficiencies required for each content area differ, and thus each instructor needs to provide a well-developed program of instruction for his or her area of study. As an example, students in social studies classes need to demonstrate skills such as the following:

1. Understanding how to use various reference and other specialized materials to locate desired information.

2. Formulating records to help the learner note the nature of assignments required along with the respective dates when such assignments are due for the teacher.

3. Designing appropriate note-taking skills when studying text and related materials as a prelude to completing any important examination.

4. Using study time wisely to accomplish definitive learning goals.

5. Reviewing information received from text materials and class lectures to help arrange ideas and concepts around a common framework of understanding.

6. Learning how to complete an examination in the most efficient manner.

7. Reviewing information effectively in preparing for an examination or giving a report.

8. Reading class text material in order to remember specific details and certain main ideas.

Though the preceding study skills competencies apply especially to social studies, they may well be applicable to other content areas as well. In the language arts, it may be necessary to use a variety of reference books to locate a poem, a fiction and/or non-fiction selection, or some other type of article. The science and math areas require special study skills, since they demand that the reader remember specific skills such as noting the sequence of steps involved in an experiment or the recalling of all the figures involved in solving a mathematics problem. The following are several principles to keep in mind for helping students build good study habits.

I. The initial step to undertake in designing any program of study skills instruction is to undertake an evaluation of each student's present competencies with regard to a predetermined list of desired study skills. The following evaluation form may be employed with secondary students. The data utilized for responding to each item will no doubt need to be obtained from careful observation of the student or the results secured from precise written assignments which demand that the student demonstrate the skill noted.

Evaluation of Study Skills*

Name _____ School _____

Grade _____ Date _____

	Satisfactory	Unsatisfactory
1. Completes school assignments by following directions accurately.	_____	_____
2. Exhibits ability to summarize various pieces of content reading material while retaining important information segments.	_____	_____
3. Knows how to construct useful outlines of sections, chapters, and complete books.	_____	_____
4. Demonstrates ability to construct well-defined and useful class notes from instructor lectures.	_____	_____
5. Notes topic sentences and understands their usefulness in securing the main idea of a section or chapter.	_____	_____
6. Senses the purpose and appropriate rate of reading which should be employed in reading a particular selection.	_____	_____
7. Selects important details and remembers those which may be needed for examinations or class discussions.	_____	_____
8. Demonstrates skill in finding the author's purpose for writing a particular piece of printed matter.	_____	_____
9. Detects the sequence of events which are outlined in a given content selection.	_____	_____
10. Selects important information from various graphic aids found in science and mathematics texts.	_____	_____

	Satisfactory	Unsatisfactory
11. Knows how to interpret the information depicted on such textbook items as maps, graphs, and charts.	_____	_____
12. Notes appropriate resources such as the *World Almanac* for assignments which require detailed information.	_____	_____
13. Follows oral directions given by the teacher regarding such aspects as assignments and projects.	_____	_____
14. Determines which words and/or phrases should be underlined when constructing class notes.	_____	_____
15. Demonstrates skill in skimming and scanning long selections for the purpose of selecting main ideas.	_____	_____
16. Knows how to utilize the various classroom encyclopedias as sources for desired data.	_____	_____
17. Exhibits an understanding of the use and importance of the table of contents, index, and glossary of a content book.	_____	_____
18. Understands and uses various appendices of content and resource books.	_____	_____
19. Knows how to outline single paragraphs, sections, and entire chapters of a given volume.	_____	_____
20. Determines the relevancy of the material being read.*	_____	_____

*From Donald C. Cushenbery, *Improving Reading Skills in the Content Area,* 1985, pp. 73–75. Courtesy of Charles C Thomas, Publisher, Springfield, Illinois.

The above inventory can be utilized at various times during the school year. To be useful in individualizing student assignments, it should be compiled as early as possible during the school year.

Another means of assessing study skills competency is through the use of a criterion-referenced group inventory. For the inventory, the secondary teacher can utilize a representative section of the class textbook that is five to seven pages in length. This segment should be read silently, and at the close of the reading each student should receive an inventory sheet that evaluates several aspects.

1. Assessment of **literal comprehension** skills from a list of several questions should be undertaken to determine ability in such areas as remembering details, finding main ideas that are stated, and following directions. The same number of questions should be used to evaluate the **interpretive** or **inferential** level. The intent of these questions should be to learn about the student's ability to draw conclusions, select the main idea, and make predictions.

2. **Reading rate** ability may be evaluated by having the student place a mark on the line of print he or she is reading at the close of a designated time period such as two or three minutes. For example, if 750 words have been read silently during a three-minute period, a reading rate of 250 words per minute is established. This rate would be considered average for most adolescent readers.

3. Using the same material from the text, the instructor can evaluate each learner's skill in implementing certain **study skill competencies.** These would include items relating to the proper use of such items as table of contents, glossary, and index. Others may include the proper assessment and interpretation of maps, graphs, and tables found on specified pages in a social studies book. Mathematics texts may contain pages of illustrations dealing with various kinds of geometric figures that may need to be interpreted. All of these aspects could be included on a grid chart that reveals the strengths and limitations of each student.

A critical score should be established for each of the subtests that have been described previously. Many reading authorities feel that a reasonable standard for each of the items described previously may be established at **80 percent proficiency.** Those students who score below the critical level need additional instruction on an individual and/or small group basis on specified study skills and/or general reading deficiencies. Additionally, the data relating to overall comprehension proficiency may lend valuable clues to the instructor relative to the suitability of the textbook. If these scores are generally *below* the critical level of 80 percent, the textbook may be too difficult; whereas, scores *above* the level may suggest that the book is too easy.

The following is a partial criterion-referenced test record sheet from Mr. Thompson's American history class.

	Details (10)	Main Ideas (8)	Graphs (8)	Tables (10)	Glossary (10)	Index (10)	Maps (12)	Rate (250)	Charts (10)
Mary S.	(6)	(5)	(7)	9	8	9	12	(175)	10
Robert K.	(6)	8	8	(7)	10	9	10	300	(6)
Mavis T.	(4)	7	(6)	10	(6)	8	(7)	260	9
Carl L.	(4)	(3)	(4)	(6)	9	(6)	11	280	10
Bill W.	(7)	(5)	(5)	8	10	9	(6)	(160)	(5)
Stacy D.	(6)	(6)	8	(5)	(5)	(5)	(6)	(180)	(4)
Wright K.	10	8	(4)	9	10	10	10	270	10
Michelle R.	(6)	(4)	(4)	(6)	(4)	(4)	(7)	(190)	9
Tony W.	(7)	(5)	(4)	9	9	10	10	350	(6)

Those scores that are circled indicate that they are below the critical level of 80 percent. A critical reading rate of 250 words per minute was established. Four of the students scored below this level and need additional help with reading at a faster rate. It is obvious that most of the class needs further help in remembering details, grasping main ideas, and interpreting graphs.

II. After study skills deficiencies have been identified, direct instruction by the instructor must be undertaken for those students who have been identified as being deficient. This instruction can take place in an individual and/or group setting. Lessons using the contract-learning concept may be used with contracts established that take into account the learner's learning style, general ability, and overall interests. Those students who have similar difficulties may be assigned contracts which have common goals.

There are numerous computer software programs that are available for use in both developmental and remedial reading settings for helping students improve all of the major reading skills, including those relating those relating to study competencies.

III. Direct instruction using study guide sheets may be utilized with the total class. The sheets can be handed to all students. Each section or item may be emphasized with appropriate oral comments used as they seem appropriate. The following is a sample sheet used by a highly successful secondary social studies instructor.

How To Develop Successful Study Habits

1. If you find a word or phrase that you don't understand, use the text glossary, an encyclopedia, or other reference book to find the correct meaning. Concentrate on the way the word is used in the context of the sentence. Many times you can figure out the meaning of the word if you understand the rest of the sentence.

2. Write your assignment carefully in your assignment notebook so you will know exactly what is expected of you.

3. Use a careful study plan such as the following:
   a. Review your notes from the previous lesson.
   b. Scan the chapter or body of material and take note of the chapter title, subtitles, pictures, and italicized and underlined words.
   c. Record questions and use them as purposes for remembering certain kinds of information. The questions may be taken from the end of the chapter or those suggested by your instructor.
   d. When you are through reading, read the questions again and see if you can remember the answers for them from the material you have read.

4. When you read, try to <u>concentrate</u> on the material that you are studying. Thinking about the football game or related matters only serve to distract you.

5. Don't try to remember a long list of small details unless you connect them together in thought units. Have a genuine purpose for each of the items you are trying to remember.

6. Look for topic sentences in paragraphs. They are usually found at the close of a body of material and serve to summarize the ideas presented previously. Read these sentences with special attention. You may want to underline them for emphasis.

7. Don't attempt to study too many subjects or books at one time.

Concentrate your attention on just two or three assignments per day or evening.

8. Place a priority on the assignments or studying that must be completed. Try to avoid being distracted by the television, parties, and other diversions. Engage in these activities only after your studying has been completed.

9. Adjust your reading rate to the purpose you have for reading. If you are reading a chapter that contains a large number of details, read at a slow, methodical rate. Conversely, if your only purpose in reading is to just remember one or two major ideas, then it is possible to skim or scan the material at 800 to 1,000 words a minute. In other words, use speed-reading techniques very sparingly and for special purposes.

10. Be sure you understand all of the details of the teacher's assignment. If you don't comprehend what is expected, ask additional questions until you are sure that you know what is needed.

11. Use a writing pad or note card and repeat writing important facts as many times as necessary to help insure that you can remember them.

12. Some students remember details better if they read them aloud. If you hear, see, and say the words, better reinforcement may take place. Don't attempt to read everything aloud, just the most important parts.

13. When taking notes in class, write down just the most important items. There is not time to write everything on the page. Review your notes carefully as soon after class as possible.

14. Your instructor has organized a special study group during the third period each day. If you have trouble studying or remembering assignments and need help with these problems, feel free to join the group.

15. There are several things you can do to help you memorize and remember specific details such as names, dates, and places. First, carefully select what you need to remember. Second, write the items on cards and place them in a card folder so you can review them when you have a few spare moments such as during a study period between classes or at the bus shelter while waiting for the school or city bus.

16. Have a scheduled time and place designated for studying your lessons. Regular, sustained study is much better than sporadic efforts at irregular times. Unless a genuine emergency occurs, stick to the time and place you have established.

IV. Secondary teachers should recognize that there are three important steps to undertake when they are helping students develop study skills. The first step is to show and demonstrate specific study strategies to the students. Model the procedure until each learner understands what he or she is to do. Let the students try the procedure under teacher supervision until they have mastered the procedure. **Second,** adequate meaningful practice should be provided until the students have firmly mastered the skill and have demonstrated clearly that they have developed this competency. **Third,** teachers must provide sufficient reinforcement to the students to insure that they develop a sense of responsibility that will provide them with consistent and effective application of skills.

CONSTRUCTING ADJUSTABLE READING RATES

During the school career of any student, he or she encounters various content classes and is expected to read the required assignments from a textbook and numerous related source books. Many learners complete the elementary grades and have developed the unfortunate habit of reading word-for-word every page of each book regardless of the structure of the volume or the nature of the reading assignment. When these students enter the secondary school, they ultimately waste hours of valuable time with slow, ineffective reading. Most of them can be helped to develop various reading rates for specific purposes; however, they must have direct instruction by the secondary teacher to build these competencies.

It is important to remember that the mark of mature readers is that they are able to select and adjust their rate of reading to the demands of the material and the assignment. He or she is flexible in rate, not only with different types of material, but also within a single selection.[1] The intent is to teach students to read all materials more flexibly rather than faster. Speed-reading is appropriate for previewing materials quickly in order to receive a general idea of the contents or for light material which is read for pleasure. It definitely is not appropriate for studying in-depth content area material.[2]

There are many reading specialists who believe that most secondary school readers can be trained to double their reading speed without a significant loss in comprehension ability. Several factors are involved in comprehension skill development; thus, the relationship between rate of reading and overall comprehension is open for serious debate. The most important concept to remember is that reading speed must be adjustable and correlated with the reader's purpose for reading a given body of material.

Recently, many students have been attracted to "speed-reading" schools. Many of these companies "guarantee" the value of their programs and promise the participants that they can increase comprehension and improve their grades. In fact, many of the program materials are geared to help readers to improve their skimming and scanning abilities. The skills may be appropriate for content areas such as literature and social studies; however, these practices have very limited value in the areas of mathematics and science where long lists of facts and figures must be remembered and processed. Despite these facts, Early[3] notes that schools continue to buy expensive equipment and parents continue to enroll their offspring in out-of-school speed-reading courses because the need for rapid reading in a print-saturated culture is very apparent. She would prefer to see school systems invest what they are budgeting for reading machines in better libraries, services to teachers, and staff development.

When building a program of flexible reading rates with secondary students, the instructor should be careful to stress the following principles.

1. The rate of reading to use depends on the reader's background of experience, the purpose one has for reading, and the relative difficulty of the print material.

2. All assignments should be previewed or surveyed before they are read in order that the correct reading rate can be ascertained.

3. Much study time can be saved by reading flexibly and using a variety of techniques.

4. Be sure you know what kinds of information you should try to remember. If you are unsure about your exact reading goals, ask your instructor for further clarification.

5. Your reading speed can be increased considerably if you try to read phrases and thought units in place of trying to read every page word-for-word.

6. Don't try to read books and materials that contain a large number of words that you cannot pronounce. Taking a large amount of time to pronounce words lowers your reading speed.

7. There are four general rates that can and should be used for various kinds of comprehension. They are detailed reading, average rate, skimming, and scanning.

Rates of Reading

Secondary students should be given specific information regarding the four rates of reading. The descriptions that follow may be used as a basis for oral discussions or printed material to be handed to learners for their consideration while building reading-rate flexibility.

I. Detailed Reading

There are many instances when the reader needs to examine each word and try to remember isolated facts and figures to solve a problem or an experiment. In mathematics this speed would be demanded to recall a sequence of figures that are to be added. A speed of 125 to 135 words per minute would be appropriate in a social studies class when a sequence of events is to be remembered for an upcoming examination. A student who has been chosen as the lead actor or actress in a school or community play needs to employ slow, deliberate, detailed reading, since he or she must say the words in the same precise manner that they are printed on the script.

II. Average Rate

There are many kinds of assignments that would be suitable for an average rate of reading of from 125 to 400 words per minute. These types of lessons require careful attention to key words, important subtopics, as well as summary and topic sentences.

The following are some examples of content area assignments that would be appropriate for using an average rate of reading.

1. To grasp the significance of a point of view which a writer promotes in a book or article.

2. To find the answer to a specific question which has been posed by the teacher in a social studies or science class.

3. To establish a correct correlation between the details and main ideas which are outlined in a section or chapter of a book or article.

4. To grasp and understand the literary style which a writer promotes in a story or novel.

5. To read and discover the major concepts which are developed in newspaper and/or magazine articles that are a part of classroom assignments.

6. To comprehend the main ideas of a selection in order to provide an oral or written summary of the material as a part of a content area

assignment. (If detailed data are required, one should read at the detailed or careful rate of reading.)[4]

III. Skimming

A natural part of previewing is to learn how to skim content material effectively. Skimming involves intensive previewing of the material to see what the reading assignment is all about, such as reading the first sentence of every paragraph. This may be accomplished by forcing a time limit on the learner of one or two minutes to read an entire selection.[5] All skimming involves fast reading; however, there are different kinds of skimming. Skimming for a number, a date, or a name can usually be done much more quickly than for the topic of a paragraph or to answer specific questions.[6]

There are numerous assignments that can be skimmed at a rapid rate of 400 to perhaps 2,000 words per minute. Some of these activities may include the following:

1. Skim the table of contents and index of the text to discover if there is information relating to ancient pyramids.

2. Skim the maps on pages 26 and 27 to find the name of the largest city in South America.

3. Skim Chapter 2 to determine if there is a discussion relating to the causes of the Spanish-American War.

4. Skim the graphs and charts on pages 26 and 34 to discover the names of the four regions in the United States that produce the most coal.

5. Skim the titles of books found in the Appendices to estimate the number and kinds of volumes dealing with the products derived from sugarcane production.

IV. Scanning

The fastest rate of reading is scanning print matter at a speed of over 2,000 words per minute. The reader attempts to find particular numbers, words, or phrases that are found among hundreds of words and phrases on a given page or several pages in a textbook or article. The mind is focused on what is being sought; it does not abstract any information, word, or phrase that does not answer the specific question the reader has in mind.[7]

When emphasizing the use of scanning techniques, the teacher should utilize reading materials at the independent reading level. Nearly every content area lends itself to scanning practice. Students should be cautioned to avoid the temptation to try to read and remember large segments of facts and concepts. For example, a biology teacher may direct the class members to "Look on page 153 and find the names of the three kinds of muscles found in the common green frog. I will allow you only ten seconds to find this information." An American history teacher may ask learners to scan pages 126–134 of their text and find the names of the first permanent settlement in Massachusetts and the date when Boston was established as a city. Miller[8] notes that timed readings of easy material in which a student tries to read predominantly in thought units is one of the best ways to increase reading rate in secondary school content classes. In timed readings, a student reads at his or her independent level or instructional level for a specific period of time such as three, five, or ten minutes.

There are many situations that may be appropriate for use with scanning techniques. The following are sample assignments that may be appropriate:

1. Open to page 58 of your text. Find the names of the first four presidents of the United States.

2. Look at the map of South America on pages 89–90. Write the names of four capital cities found on that continent.

3. Notice the map of the continental United States on pages 50–51. What are the names of two mountain peaks that are over 10,000 feet in altitude?

4. Read the definitions of the word "institute" on page 98 of the class dictionary. Which definition applies to "institute" as it appears in this sentence? **John spent the evening at the Art Institute.**

In summary, scanning is the most rapid of all reading rates and should be used when the goal is the location of a specific word, phrase, or number that constitutes the answer to a specific question.

Procedures for Improving Reading Rate

Content teachers can institute various strategies and practices for helping their students develop more flexible reading rates. There are numerous informal classroom practices that can be employed along with commercial mechanical devices. The degree of improvement which may be realized by any given student depends on several factors such as learner motivation, general reading ability, age of the student, and the amount of time devoted to such activities. A description of both informal and commercial strategies is included in the next two subsections.

Informal Classroom Techniques

1. Each student should be provided with a large amount of reading material at his or her independent reading level. The teacher instructs the members of the class to read consciously faster than they normally do. At a signal the entire group begins simultaneously to read. The teacher records 10-second intervals on the chalkboard. When the reader completes a designated selection, the student notes the number of 10-second intervals written on the board and calculates his or her reading rate.[9]

2. A series of timed reading exercises may be prepared by the teacher. For secondary students, the first exercise may involve 800 words; the second, 1,100 words; the third, 1,500 words, etc., with each succeeding passage containing an ever-increasing number of words. A universal time span should be established for all passages. The goal for each student should be to read ever-increasing longer passages with no additional reading time permitted.

3. Rate improvement cannot be built on inadequate word-identification and word-recognition skills. It cannot be built on an experimental background that keeps the reader from understanding what he or she is reading. It cannot be built upon immaturity in intellectual development.[10] Those students who have basic reading skill deficiencies such as those mentioned previously must be given appropriate remedial instructional help to alleviate these difficulties before serious attention is given to formal reading-rate improvement programs.

4. Direct instruction should be provided to help students improve their competency in reading materials in thought and phrase units rather than word-for-word methods. A simple tachistoscope device may be used to expose a line of print at a time. A 4-by-6-inch card with an opening cut for a single line of a page should be appropriate. The student can move the card down the page at progressively faster rates. A card can also be utilized as a pacing device by moving it down the page and covering lines of print at increasing speeds.

Commercial Devices

There are numerous tachistoscope and controlled reading devices available for helping students increase reading rate. The tachistoscope devices include the *Flash-X* (E.D.L., Inc.), the *Phrase-Flasher* (Reading Laboratory), and the *Pocket-Tac* (Reading Institute). The previous instruments are individual hand-held models. There are machines that can be used with a large class or group of students. These include the *Craig Reader* (Creative Curriculum) and the *Controlled Reader* (EDL). Other mechanical machines act as pacers that cover lines of print with a plastic bar or a beam of light. Examples of these instruments include the *Reading Rateometer* (AVR) and the *Shadowscope Reading Pace* (Psychotechnics). There is a considerable amount of disagreement among reading authorities regarding the amount of transfer of rate improvement that may be expected from the extensive use of such devices.

USING READING–STUDY STRATEGIES

Many students have very limited abilities to read numerous pages of print material and remember a significant amount of data and concepts. By and large, secondary teachers have tended to use traditional methods such as large group instruction, lectures, teacher-directed homework, and periodic examinations to achieve the basic reading goal of comprehension building. By contrast, Naomi Zigmond and others[11] conducted a research study and discovered that low achieving students actually accomplish much more learning when small group instruction is used along with cooperative learning and the direct face-to-face participation of students and teachers. It is the contention of a number of reading authorities that secondary teachers must help students build rather precise strategies or formulas to help them deal appropriately with voluminous text materials and the wide range of reading abilities present within any large class.

Reading strategies instruction enables the student to become more aware and sensitive to the nature and kind of reading topics about to be studied, along with some definitive knowledge concerning what aspects of the reading matter are important to remember in detail and what can be skimmed or scanned for general impressions. Some formulas emphasize pre-reading strategies to help the learner bridge the gap between the learner's present background of experience and what will be expected when the pending assignment is read and comprehended.

They also result in the student's improvement in the areas of note taking, outlining, organizing, and integrating assigned readings. The strategies improve comprehension generally and greatly facilitate growth with regard to motivation and interest in reading. There are many different reading-study formulas, and the one chosen by a given secondary teacher to be emphasized should depend on the age of the students, instructional objectives, and the overall reading abilities of the affected students.

There are several notable reading strategies that are employed by secondary teachers. These include the **SQ3R technique**, the **R.E.A.P. Procedure**, the **DRTA activity method**, and the **MULTIPASS strategy**. Each of these is described below.

I. Francis Robinson[12] developed the **SQ3R technique** and is described in a famous volume that he authored in 1961. The procedures consist of five basic stages.

A. Survey. There are numerous strategies included in the survey of a chapter. They consist of such items as the following:

1. **Read the chapter title, introduction, subtopics, and summary to get a clear understanding of the nature of the topics presented. By surveying the material carefully, the reader can secure appropriate background of information relative to the concepts discussed and how these subjects are interrelated.**

2. **Try to picture an overall outline of the material and construct a structured overview of the topics and thus draw relationships that appear to exist between and among various subject categories. If the material is surveyed carefully, the learner can gain appropriate readiness for understanding and remembering important concepts and ideas.**

B. Question. If adequate comprehension is to be obtained, the student must develop purposes for reading. The questions can be formulated by looking at the main headings and restructuring the titles into questions. The learner may also utilize any guiding questions supplied by the textbook author and found at the beginning or close of the chapter.

C. Read. During the silent reading, the learner should use the questions as guides to determine which types of information to remember and assimilate. The printed matter supplied for reading should be at the

Establishing Significant Study Skills Competencies   105

instructional reading level demonstrated by the student. Careful observation of the student during silent reading may reveal undesirable reading habits that may be corrected through individualized lessons.

D. Recite. Following the silent reading, the student should attempt to recall the answers to the questions or purposes established in step 2. If proper responses cannot be formulated, a careful rereading of portions of the reading material may be necessary.

E. Review. At this stage the entire chapter should be reviewed with a construction of an outline undertaken to help recall the most important details and interpretive data. Application and correlation of the material just read should be made. Extension reading should be taken to supply additional information and greater depth to the total body of knowledge. The total review should be helpful to the student when preparing for a test.

II. Eanet and Manzo[13] developed a very valuable strategy called R.E.A.P. for students who need to develop effective comprehension and improve study skills. There are four basic steps to the procedure:

> R—Read the assigned material and try to select the main idea(s) which the author(s) sought to project to the reader.
>
> E—Encode the main ideas and rewrite these data into the vocabulary and thought processes of the learner.
>
> A—Annotate the information to provide a meaningful summary for remembering data for a test or sharing with the teacher or fellow classmates as the occasion demands.
>
> P—Ponder the material and determine the thesis of the writer's message and how it relates to the general body of information already known and understood about a topic.

III. Russell Stauffer[14] constructed a four-step process called the **Directed Reading-Thinking Activity** method for helping students develop purposes and strategies for improving overall comprehension when reading a selection. The *first* step consists of identifying purposes or questions for understanding silent reading. *Second,* the learner must be advised to adjust his or her reading rate to correlate with the reading purposes and difficulty of the reading material. *Third,* the instructor is obliged to observe the silent reading habits of each student in order to evaluate any reading difficulties as a preface to planning remedial help. *Fourth,* comprehension skills are developed through the use of numerous skill-building activities. The D.R.T.A. procedure should always involve the learner directly in each step of the strategy.

IV. Jean Schumaker and others[15] recently developed the **MULTIPASS** strategy for studying efficiently and improving overall reading comprehension. The three steps in the plan are **survey, size-up,** and **sort-out.** During the **survey** stage, the reader is encouraged to take a close look at the title and subtitles of the chapter and try to gather the main ideas that are presented. The formulation of appropriate questions and purposes for reading is also encouraged. The **size-up** step is to be used for a general reading of the assigned material to obtain sufficient data and concepts to satisfy the purposes and questions established during the survey stage. The last step, **sort-out,** entails the evaluation and sorting of information just read to allow the secondary students to test themselves over the material read and reviewed. The authors utilized the approach with large groups of low achieving and learning disabled students at the high school level and found that they were able to dramatically improve their levels of textbook comprehension while using the strategy.

Before *any* strategy is undertaken with any group of secondary students, the instructor should remember the following guidelines or principles.

1. **Explain** the strategy in its entirety by pointing out each step carefully and how it relates to the total plan. A carefully prepared handout that explains the plan may be useful to allow students to review the material at a later time when reading and studying at home or the school library.

2. **Demonstrate** the plan through the use of oral reading, display of overhead transparencies, and printed materials. Point out important text materials by the use of heavy black type, italicized letters, and/or underlining techniques. Model the procedures utilizing the course text and other required print materials. Emphasize any "do's" and "don'ts" that should be remembered when employing the techniques.

3. Ask students to **rehearse** the plan through the use of current materials and actual classroom assignments. They should be encouraged to share any problems or concerns they may have with the procedures so they can be accommodated before further studying is undertaken.

4. Students should **evaluate** the strengths and limitations of the plan through the use of oral discussions and/or a printed evaluation form. A careful study of the evaluation data should be of significant help to the instructor for deciding what plan is most helpful for individual learners.

·In summary, reading-study strategies can be very helpful to students of all ability levels as they study and attempt to comprehend at a maximum level. A study plan combined with a flexible reading rate can prove to be a significant learning advantage for the total student body.

BUILDING NOTE-TAKING TECHNIQUES

A close inspection of the words, phrases, and sentences found in the notebooks of the average secondary student often reveals a very disorganized procedure for taking notes from textbook readings and class lectures. In many instances, the notes are placed in one central location without regard to the applicable subject, while others are written on cards or small pieces of paper. Some students have no doubt lost some of the notes taken the week before. This type of note-taking makes remembering details for tests and reports very difficult. Students who have inefficient note-taking skills need direct systematic help from secondary content teachers as they improve in these areas.

The following are several teacher-tested methods for helping learners improve their note-taking skills:

1. The instructor should give *a typical lecture* relating to a topic of wide interest to the students. Students should be advised to employ their "usual" method of note taking. When the lecture is completed, the instructor should display a transparency on the classroom screen that shows a "model" set of notes which has been compiled by the teacher. An explanation should be given relative to the importance of each item on the screen. A playback of the original lecture may be conducted while the notes are being explained. These procedures allow the students to see the *correct* note-taking practices unfold before them as they hear the lecture from the tape. The plan can be repeated as many times as necessary until a satisfactory level of note-taking proficiency has been attained.

2. One of the major methods to use for taking effective notes is to devise *a form of outlining* that is clear and consistent. A time order outline such as the following may be constructed:

> Title: Specific steps are followed in a
> controlled experiment.
> I. A question is asked.
> II. A hypothesis is formulated.
> III. A plan of attack is followed.
> A. First . . .
> B. Second . . .
> C. Third . . .

IV. Results are acted upon.
   A. Results are observed.
   B. Results are tabulated.
   C. Results are interpreted.[16]

Students should be sure they understand the complete organizational pattern and what kinds of information should be placed at various points. The first and most basic concept is for the student to see the structure of the information which may involve paragraph analysis and chapter or unit organization in the textbook. The other is the more mechanical skill of outline form. Students may learn the basic form through direct instruction followed by guidance in applying it to selected passages.[17]

3. A *note-taking system for learning* (NSL) was devised by Palmatier[18] and has been used widely by many students. The plan is easy to follow and consists of the following steps:

   a. Use only one side of a page of wide-lined 8½-by-11-inch notebook paper.
   b. Lecture notes should be placed only to the right side of the margin on the sheet.
   c. Labels should be placed to the left of the margin line with notations that correspond with the information included written in the corresponding space to the right of the line.
   d. Reading notes should be compiled on separate sheets of paper and inserted in proper places among the lecture notes so coordination is achieved.

4. When a student is reading texts and other related assignments, they should develop a skillful ability to take notes by *summarizing*. This technique can be demonstrated by the teacher placing a paragraph or a section of the textbook on a transparency and projecting it on the classroom screen. Students should be asked to summarize the script in a defined limit of words or sentences. Emphasize the importance of giving close attention to topic sentences, italicized words, and words in bold type. They may wish to share their summaries and gain an understanding of what most students think are the important portions of the material.

Note-taking is a skill that is not well developed by many secondary students. Few learners are prepared for the rigorous assignments and lectures that they regularly encounter when they begin their college experiences. While many young people can develop efficient note-taking skills in a group setting, some of them will need individual instruction in a tutorial setting. This type of instruction may take place in the school's reading-study center if the content teacher cannot arrange such instruction. The suggestions included in the previous section may be incorporated in most group class settings.

SUMMARY

Many secondary students have not mastered the ability to study efficiently and thus become discouraged and defeated in the learning environment. As noted at the beginning of this chapter, there are a large number of competencies that must be developed. Adjusting the rate of reading according to one's reading purposes is a valuable skill to develop. Reading-study strategies are of immense help for reading and understanding large assignment segments. Helping learners build note-taking skills to assimilate significant concepts drawn from lectures and print media must be stressed by all secondary teachers.

REFERENCES

1. Shepherd, David L. *Comprehensive High School Reading Methods* (Second Edition). Columbus, Charles E. Merrill, 1978, p. 135.
2. Askov, Eunice N. and Karlyn Kamm. *Study Skills in the Content Areas.* Boston, Allyn and Bacon, 1982, p. 80.
3. Early, Margaret. *Reading to Learn in Grades 5 to 12.* New York, Harcourt Brace Jovanovich, 1984, p. 429.
4. Cushenbery, Donald C. *Improving Reading Skills in the Content Areas.* Springfield, Charles C Thomas, Publisher, 1985, p. 88.
5. Vacca, Richard T. and JoAnne L. Vacca. *Content Area Reading* (Second Edition). Boston, Little, Brown, 1986, p. 264.
6. Rubin, Dorothy. *Diagnosis and Correction in Reading Instruction.* New York, Holt, Rinehart and Winston, 1982, p. 271.
7. McNeil, John D., Lisbeth Donant, and Marvin C. Alkin. *How to Teach Reading Successfully.* Boston, Little, Brown, 1980, p. 167.
8. Miller, Wilma H. *Teaching Reading in the Secondary School.* Springfield, Charles C Thomas, Publisher, 1974, p. 143.
9. Harris, Larry A. and Carl B. Smith. *Reading Instruction Diagnostic Teaching in the Classroom.* New York, Macmillan Publishing Company, 1986, p. 361.
10. Dechant, Emerald V. and Henry P. Smith. *Psychology in Teaching Reading* (Second Edition). Englewood Cliffs, Prentice-Hall, 1977, p. 279.
11. Zigmond, Naomi, and others, "Teaching Learning Disabled Students at the

Secondary School Level: What Research Says to Teachers." *Learning Disabilities Focus,* V. 1 (Spring, 1986), pp. 108–115.

12. Robinson, Frances P. *Effective Study* (Revised Edition). New York, Harper and Row, 1961.

13. Eanet, Marilyn and Anthony V. Manzo, "REAP—A Strategy for Improving Reading/ Writing/Study Skills." *Journal of Reading,* V. 19 (May, 1976), pp. 647–652.

14. Stauffer, Russell G. *Directing the Reading Thinking Process.* New York, Harper and Row, 1975.

15. Schumaker, Jean and others, "MULTIPASS: A Learning Strategy for Improving Reading Comprehension." *Learning Disability Quarterly,* V. 5 (Summer, 1982), pp. 295–304.

16. Burmeister, Lou E. *Reading Strategies for Secondary School Teachers.* Reading, Addison-Wesley Publishing Company, 1974, p. 165.

17. David L. Shepherd, *High School Reading,* p. 115.

18. Palmatier, R. "A Note-Taking System for Learning." *Journal of Reading* (January, 1973), pp. 36–39.

Chapter VI

DEVELOPING AND PROMOTING
READING INTERESTS

One of the chief functions of any teacher is that of developing and promoting the reading interests of students. A significant question asked by many teachers and members of the lay public is "Why do some students build an effective base of reading skills and are motivated to read widely while others seem to dislike reading activities?" There are various reasons why some learners fail to read at an acceptable level with one of them being a general lack of motivation.

A casual observation of any secondary content class in session often reveals that there are significant numbers of students reading with enthusiasm and interest, while others appear to dislike lessons that require reading assignments. Obviously, the latter students need to be motivated to read through the use of numerous strategies available to classroom teachers.

To lend valuable help to secondary teachers for developing and promoting reading interests, the following topics are discussed in this chapter: evaluating reading interests; principles for building motivation; procedures for motivating all readers; and effective use of computerized instruction for building lifelong reading interests. A summary and a body of references conclude the chapter.

EVALUATING READING INTERESTS

One of the most significant means of motivating students to read is evaluating each student's level of reading interests and building a curriculum of studies that will correlate with these interests. The use of structured, required assignments by teachers without regard to student interests may, in fact, tend to eliminate the enjoyment and motivation that should encompass the reading act. Karlin[1] notes that high school students are often in a period of rebellion and seek independence and individuality. While they enjoy identifying with characters they recognize, they often resent books that have been especially written for them and want volumes that address adult problems.

A reading program for secondary students may be deemed worthwhile when there is direct evidence that numerous students turn to many books and journals and read them freely for information and sheer relaxation. At that point, these learners will find that reading is as enjoyable as an athletic contest or a school dance. For this situation to develop, reading activities must be related to the identified interests and preferences of students.

It is helpful to assess the reading interests of students and try to correlate assignments and class activities with the types of books they prefer. Burmeister[2] notes that it is important to remember that chronological age, rather than mental age (or IQ), is a major factor in determining a student's reading interests. Bright students tend to enjoy the same types of stories as do average students of the same chronological age. Young adolescents usually seek out adult fiction and like stories about young people their own age.

There are numerous ways of collecting data regarding the individual and collective reading interests of secondary students. The administration of a reading interest inventory to be completed by all students at the beginning of the school year should lend important guidance to the secondary content teacher.

The following is a sample of an interest inventory utilized by one teacher.

Reading Interest Inventory

Name _____   Class _____

1. List the names of three magazines that you read on a regular basis.

   _____

   _____

2. When you read magazines, what kinds of articles do you like best?

   _____   _____

   _____   _____

   _____   _____

3. Do you read a newspaper more than once a week?
   _____ Yes _____ No

When you read a newspaper, what parts are your favorites?
Put the letter "A" in front of the part of the newspaper what
you normally read first. Place the letter "B" in front of the
part you read second. Place the letter "C" if you never read
the section.

____ Fashions   ____ Advertisements
____ Front-page news   ____ Financial news
____ Sports pages   ____ Entertainment
____ Cartoons   ____ Crossword puzzles
____ Astrology   ____ "Help-wanted" ads

4. Name one or more books that you have read completely
    during the past two or three years that *have not* been
    assigned to be read by a teacher.

    _____   _____
    _____   _____
    _____   _____

5. Which of the following persons do you consult *first* for
    suggestions relating to interesting books to read? Place a
    number 1 in front of the person's name who influences you
    to the greatest degree. Place a number 2 for the person who
    has the least influence.

    ____ English teacher   ____ History teacher
    ____ Friends   ____ Parents
    ____ Librarian   ____ Brother and/or sister

6. The following are names of books that are available in our
    school library. Pretend that you *have not* read them and
    they *have not* been assigned to be read by one of your
    teachers. Place a check mark in front of four books that you
    might check out to read for fun and enjoyment.

    __ *How to Read Faster and Better*   __ *Famous Bank Robberies*
    __ *Washington Redskins:*   __ *America's Next President*
       National Champions   __ *Exploring the Grand Canyon*
    __ *Avoiding the AIDS Epidemic*   __ *1000 Ways to Earn Money*
    __ *The Vanishing Robber*   __ *Caught in a Blizzard*
    __ *The Stock Market Crash of 1987*   __ *A Ride in a Rocket*
    __ *Occupations of the Future*   __ *An Encyclopedia of*
    __ *The Police Roadblock*   *America's Colleges*

___ *Improve Your Personality*   ___ *Three New Ways to Success*
___ *Heroes of the World Series*   ___ *Nelson's Guide to Used Cars*
___ *How to Study Efficiently*   ___ *The Best of Comedy*
___ *Take Care of Your Health*   ___ *Ten Essentials for Success*

In addition to a reading interest inventory, a teacher-made instrument may be utilized to gain ideas regarding the present attitudes of students about reading in general. The results of the questionnaire may be useful for structuring class activities to enhance reading interests.

<u>Reading Attitudes Inventory</u>

Name _____ Date _____

Read the following statements. If you believe that the statement is *true* about you, place a "+" sign on the blank. If it is *not true,* place an "o" sign on the blank.

_____ 1. I read at least part of some newspaper each day.
_____ 2. Once I start reading a book, I generally keep going until I finish it.
_____ 3. I would rather read than watch television programs.
_____ 4. Reading is one of my favorite activities.
_____ 5. I enjoy reading aloud in class.
_____ 6. If I am through reading assignments during study periods, I generally start reading a novel or short story.
_____ 7. When I am reading a book, I pay more attention to the pictures than I do the sentences and paragraphs.
_____ 8. I don't usually go to the library or media center unless I plan to read *assigned* books and articles.
_____ 9. I like to read books for fun and pleasure.
_____ 10. If I read a good book, I usually tell a friend about it so he or she can read the book as well.
_____ 11. I find most library books to be quite dull and uninteresting.
_____ 12. Teachers should not require any kind of book reports.
_____ 13. I enjoy reading books at home after I have completed my homework.
_____ 14. Reading allows me to share the adventures, thoughts, and ideas of many other people.

(In analyzing the responses to the above statements, one should normally expect to find positive responses for all items except numbers 7, 8, 11, and 12.)

There are numerous other informal procedures that can be used to evaluate reading interests. These may include the following.

1. Listen to oral comments made by students during routine class discussions to grasp the degree and level of reading interests displayed by individual learners.

2. Place numerous interesting books from the library on a table in the classroom and invite students to voluntarily read and report on books of their choice. Note the identity of the learners who check out books and those who show little, if any, desire to read.

PRINCIPLES FOR BUILDING MOTIVATION

Motivation is an essential ingredient in any learning process. If basic reading interests are to be fostered, motivation must be the heart of all teaching strategies. Most secondary students want to succeed and possess inherent motivators of the desire for success and achievement. Discouraged secondary instructors may conclude that since a certain student has little or no interest in reading, he or she prefers to become a failure. The building of motivation is a challenging responsibility, since each learner requires a different set of strategies to generate reading desires. Many students are not motivated to read a book or article for the simple purpose of passing a test. Other approaches must be utilized. Certain decisions, actions, concepts, and principles must be established.

First, students must be situated in a classroom environment that will cause them to want to read widely. Too many secondary instructors require such extensive textbook assignments that the readers never have a spare moment to pursue personal reading interests. Motivation for many learners will never be realized until they have books available to them that are written on several difficulty levels and may be used on a *voluntary* basis. Research studies indicate that some readers will read certain volumes even if a test is not administered over the material.

Second, high school teachers need to remember that very few students really want to fail. It is entirely possible for instructors to construct a meaningful learning environment and establish both intrinsic and extrinsic award systems that provide for success when undertaking reading assignments. For example, the use of an experiment or a media device may be a sufficient stimulus to cause a student to want to read more widely for information. Perhaps readers may be motivated to read to prove a contention that they may hold. They feel they have been awarded for their efforts when they are asked to share their data with the rest of the class.

Third, **a decision must be made at the outset regarding whether or not a student CAN read efficiently.** Perhaps there may be definitive physical and/or emotional problems that may be preventing the young person from realizing success. The use of illegal drugs may be a significant deterrent to reading. Some research study data show that at least 65 percent of all young people experiment with such drugs at least once before the age of 18. A complete medical and/or psychological evaluation may need to be conducted to assess any possible limitations. No one can be motivated to accomplish tasks that are beyond the realm of reasonable expectations. A program of rehabilitation may be undertaken through the careful correlation of the efforts of classroom teachers, parents, therapists, and medical professions.

Fourth, **adequate attention must be given to reading assignments that relate to the immediate needs of the students such as passing a driver's test, reading advertisements for jobs, and reading and completing job application forms.** The previous activities are goals pursued by many adolescents and thus are natural springboards for reading assignments. The state driver's license manual may be utilized as recommended reading material. The intensive study of various job application forms may emphasize how to complete the forms in the best way to help insure success for securing desired employment to earn money to buy an automobile. These are everyday reading needs of secondary students and can provide an important motive for young people to read. Teachers should emphasize the reading assignments given are related to the types of reading skills that readers will need when they complete their formal schooling.

Fifth, **secondary content teachers must realize that there are other conditions and situations in the environment of a student that can diminish one's motivation level for reading and learning.** Analyzing the schedule of typical adolescents may show that they watch a considerable number of television programs, participate in sports, and engage in social activities. Some authorities have discovered that many students may spend as many as 40 hours per week watching television shows. Several of them may think that the rewards for participating in sports and related activities outweigh the benefits of engaging in extensive reading activities. One of the most important goals of a secondary content teacher is to persuade learners that they can complete extensive reading and engage in school functions as well.

Sixth, secondary instructors should keep in mind that they may be the most influential role model for many of their students. Too many readers come from homes where parents are unmotivated and reading books and articles has a low priority. (In some areas of the country the rate of functional illiteracy among parents is at a 35 to 45 percent rate of the total population. They may be unable to model good reading.) In order for them to be motivated, they need the exposure of teachers who project the impression by word and deed that reading is an enjoyable and highly interesting activity.

Seventh, immediate and specific feedback on tests and assignments is an important element in motivation. One researcher[3] conducted an investigation utilizing 74 teachers of grades 7–12, who were asked to administer an objective test to their classes. They scored the tests and randomly assigned the tests to one of three groups. The first group of papers had the score and grade noted on the top side of the test. The second group of papers received the usual scores plus general positive statements such as "Liked your answers. Keep going." The third group received scores, grades, and very specific comments of a positive nature relating to individual sections. *A later follow-up of a second test showed that the best performances were obtained by those who had been in the third group on the first test, regardless of their grade level or past academic achievement.* Secondary teachers would be well advised to remember that a high level of motivation can be obtained if grading is *immediate* and *detailed.* Positive comments should be made when they are appropriate.

In summary, the role of motivation must be classified as an important factor for students who desire to excel in developmental, corrective, and remedial reading endeavors. They must feel a need to read and achieve a high level of success if they are to be successful. The seven principles just discussed should be practiced by secondary teachers if motivation for reading is to become a part of the total body of classroom activities.

PROCEDURES FOR MOTIVATING ALL READERS

Motivation often explains why one student completes a reading assignment and another does not. Intelligence, language facility, cultural background, and other such factors may differ *insignificantly* for the two students; *however,* motivational differences may be the *significant* factor.

Motivation is an individual need that causes a learner to do something that will result in satisfaction. There are numerous strategies that may be undertaken by secondary teachers to affect, negatively or positively, the motivational level of students to read with interest and vigor. With respect to negative aspects, Claunch and Nutt[4] note that non-readers are made, not born, and there are some definitive ways of turning off adolescent readers. A sampling of such directives include the following.

- "Only hardback books may be used for your book report." (Paperback books may be "dirty.")
- "You may not read any more of the type of books you've been reading for book reports." (Your taste "stinks".)
- "You may not read any books by this author." (I don't agree with this author.)
- "Your books must contain more than 100 pages." (There is a magic number that guarantees quality writing.)
- "Read three books and write reports on them in the next four weeks." (I need more grades for this grading period.)

Secondary teachers need to attempt to motivate students to read through the use of one or more positive approaches such as the following:

1. Instructors should always be warm, non-threatening, and non-punitive partners in the learning process. They learn to listen and watch for and try to interpret non-verbal clues. They do not make false promises, since what happens to students will result much more from their behavior than from teachers.[5]

2. Reading interests should be promoted by every content teacher. *First,* teachers must learn about the factors that correlate with interest formations. *Second,* they should learn about the interest patterns that are typical of the grade level taught. *Third,* a study must be made of the individual interests of each student (through the use of the interest inventory described earlier). *Fourth,* teachers must use every opportunity to develop and extend interest.[6]

3. Developing a cheerful and inviting classroom environment is conducive for building reading interests of students. A table could be placed in one corner of the room where various resource books from a given content area are displayed. The books should be rotated with newer volumes in evidence on a regular basis. Students should be invited to review one or more books during the course of the semester or school year.

4. Business and other community leaders may be invited to speak to

the students regarding new books or articles that they have read or published. This type of activity creates the impression that "important" people read books and enjoy the experience.

5. Several companies produce tapes and computer software which serve to introduce books that have been written on various subjects. Some of the programs give a short introduction to the material, pose questions to arouse interest, and invite learners to read the total volume. Several of the companies which produce these kinds of programs advertise in professional journals.

6. Many content teachers make use of bibliotherapy to motivate reluctant readers to read and enjoy selected books. While using this technique, the teacher selects books which students might like to read because of a difficult problem or challenge they are confronting. For example, *Empty Chair* (Harper, 1978) or *Learning to Say Good-Bye — When a Parent Dies* (MacMillan, 1976) may be appropriate for students who have experienced the death of a parent. Those who are children of divorced parents may want to read *How Does It Feel When Your Parents Get Divorced* (Messner, 1977) or *Two Special Cards* (Harcourt, 1976). Those who are afflicted with drug or alcohol problems may wish to read *It Aint All For Nothin'* (Viking, 1978) or *Something Left to Lose* (Knopf, 1976). *Leo, the Late Bloomer* (Scholastic, 1981) and *How I Faded Away* (Whitman, 1976) may be useful for those readers who have a poor self-concept.

There are several sources available for finding information about books to be used for bibliotherapy purposes. One of the most useful volumes is *Bookfinder* which is published by American Guidance Services, Inc., Circle Pines, Minnesota 55014.

7. There are a large number of magazines and book clubs available for students of varying ages. Many of these sources contain selections which are very interesting reading material for all pupils, especially those who are unmotivated and not inspired to read. A listing of many of these selections can be obtained from media specialists.

8. Many local and state educational agencies sponsor reading clubs for both elementary and secondary students. In most cases, certificates are issued to students after they have read a certain number of books. Content teachers should become informed about the clubs and urge students to participate actively in such organizations.[7]

9. Morale has a significant relationship to motivation. Most people have heard about morale as an important facet of how well a young man or woman succeeds in the armed forces. The relationship is just as

important to the students who are enrolled in the secondary school. Learners with a low level of morale normally don't endeavor to accomplish much, because they are not self-assured and seem never to be of the opinion that what they are doing is vital. Secondary teachers need to understand that morale is composed of three important factors: *self-assurance, positive understanding of the task,* and *belief in a successful conclusion.* Those students who are assured of their ability tend to try harder and work longer than a person without this feeling. They also need to believe in the assignment given to them and that it is very possible for them to work longer and harder and finish a task to its completion.

10. Highly successful secondary teachers use *progress plotting* as a motivational tool, since some studies show that the reading results obtained by *all* levels of students are maximized when they see great value in the goal they are trying to reach. The progress plotter can be individual charts or records on which the learner records the number of items accomplished and the degree of success realized. Records may include the number of lessons completed, names of resource books consulted, increase in speed of reading, and new vocabulary words learned during a unit or chapter studied.

11. Some relatively unmotivated students need supervised in-class reading as a follow-up to a careful assignment that makes clear to students:

    a. How the assigned reading connects with what they already know;

    b. What their purposes are and why they are important;

    c. What strategies they should use to identify and remember important information.

These steps provide direction to the learner and establish a road map that allows him or her to realize success through a carefully designed program of studies. Short-term goals seem reachable and help provide for a feeling of "reaching the top." The sensitive teacher allows as many assignment choices as possible by balancing "electives" with "requirements."[8]

12. One avenue frequently overlooked for building motivation of adolescents is that of providing a handbook or bulletin to parents that outlines some attitudes and procedures that should be undertaken in the home. Parents are often unskilled in the knowledge of constructing favorable reading attitudes and need advice on what they can do. The following suggestions may be included in such a publication.

    a. Try to be a positive role model for your child by sharing books and articles with them that you have read recently.

    b. Provide an adequate work and study area in your home for your son or daughter where distractions can be kept to a minimum.

    c. Invest in books, magazines, and a reputable set of encyclopedias if possible. If such materials are easily available, they will be used by most adolescents.

    d. Visit the public library <u>with</u> your child and engage in reading activities while he or she is reading or studying.

13. A powerful motivational device is that of providing students with a "taste" of what to expect if they read a certain selection or book. Some instructors use "teasers" that consist of shortened versions from the first part of a volume and which give a hint about the exciting story that is about to unfold. Some companies have produced these types of materials for use with their books and lessons. Several of these are mentioned in advertisements in professional journals.

14. The use of guest speakers during certain class periods can have a very positive effect on building reading interests. It would be ideal to have authors speak. As noted earlier, there are other persons who may have a stimulating influence on students. Such individuals may include scientists, local business persons, and government officials who may choose to show films or display posters and other print material relating to books, magazines, and articles pertaining to various subjects. These people may serve as distinguished role models for the students, since they can readily see that "important" people are readers.

One of the most obvious resource speakers is the school librarian or media specialist. This person can be of significant help in motivating students in secondary content classes by reviewing some of the new books that have been recently added to the library collection. These volumes may be of both fictional and non-fictional types. Special attention may be given to resource books such as a new set of encyclopedias or almanacs of various types. Other supplementary materials which could be demonstrated include historical novels, biographies of famous persons such as presidents, scientists, and inventors, and reproductions of original items such as old newspapers and magazines. The secondary instructor should accompany the students to the media center during a designated future time, during which time the director could help the students locate the books and materials mentioned during his/her class-room visit.

15. A very natural aspect of raising the motivational level of any learner is that of the teacher providing a sufficient body of incentives or rewards for those students who reach certain goals or heights of achievement. Tangible awards may consist of framed certificates such as "Outstanding Literature Award" or "Center Hills Reading Achievement Award." These could be given for reading a certain number of books in given categories. If a term or unit paper is required, a higher grade could be assigned to those students who utilize a certain minimum number of sources. Extra credit may be given to secondary students who read and utilize books and materials that are in excess of a required minimum assignment.

16. Harriet Smith,[9] a teacher in the Springfield Senior High School, Philadelphia, Pennsylvania, undertook a creative motivational project to award those good students—the ones who often get lost in between the best athlete and merit scholar awards, the quietly competent who looked at her talk and asked questions that showed that something was coming through. Her strategy was a simple one, but it worked. She wrote 10 short letters to the parents of outstanding students. She told parents how much she enjoyed their children and what special qualities made each a name to remember. This type of recognition goes a long way toward reinforcing positive behavior. The writer carries happier memories of the school year because the "top 10 letters" forced her, literally, to end the term on a positive note.

In summary, one of the most challenging tasks confronting the content teacher is that of motivating students to read various print media. Society dictates that students must become literate in the language arts areas, especially reading. The degree to which a learner becomes a highly proficient reader is somewhat dependent on the degree of motivation received from teachers, parents, and peers.

Teachers need to be good role models and provide an academic setting which will allow success to be possible for the reader. Sufficient awards of both an intrinsic and extrinsic nature should be made available. There are various strategies described in the previous section which should be of significant help to secondary content teachers in building levels of motivation for numerous reading assignments.

EFFECTIVE USE OF COMPUTERIZED INSTRUCTION FOR BUILDING LIFELONG READING INTERESTS

As noted in earlier sections, there are many publishers and manufacturers who have developed significant pieces of computer-friendly programs. Secondary teachers may employ software for any one or more of the following purposes for building lifelong reading interests.

Leading Drill and Practice Programs

These lessons can be used for those students who need additional practice. The Minnesota Educational Computing Corporation markets software for the construction of these types of lessons or formulating tests to fit classroom-designed activities and utilizes the Apple computer. Other lessons include *Advanced Reading Comprehension* (Educulture, Inc.), *Preparing for the SAT* (Houghton Mifflin), and *Returning to Reading Coursework* (Media Basics).

Secondary students need to become familiar with *word processing programs* for preparation of summaries, term papers, and other assignments. Some of the better materials are *Bank Street Writer* (Scholastic) and *Magic Slate* (Sunburst Communications). These programs are quite useful for creative writing and especially language experience activities. If a large monitor is available, the material can be directly entered on the computer, rather than on the chalkboard, and can be easily modified according to suggestions given during class discussion, resulting in a well-organized neat handout that can be printed and duplicated for the students' use.[10]

Computer programs to *build interest* and *enrich reading knowledge* can be utilized satisfactorily with students at all ability levels. The *Oregon Trail* program (MECC), the *Stepping Stones* program (Flaron), and the *Great Science Knowledge Race* (Cambridge Development Laboratory) are excellent examples of high interest reading material for independent study activities. These lessons are especially helpful and challenging for gifted students for use in conducting research and writing class reports and papers. The *Oregon Trail* lessons add many details and concepts to the information found in a typical American history book. The *Stepping Stones* program helps students to work independently to improve critical reading and language skills while they also gain insight into the world of work. The *Great Science Knowledge Race* includes challenging activities dealing with enrichment activities in life science, physical science, and earth science.

As noted earlier, drill and practice programs are important segments of computer instruction. They comprise much of the teaching materials inventory available for computer use. In the area of interest building, guided and independent practice are necessary to consolidate concepts and to provide opportunities for overlearning and automaticity. These programs allow teachers to look to software to provide individualized practice. They allow secondary students to practice what has been taught.[11] There are a number of inherent advantages for using the computer to provide drill and practice activities for various learners. Balajthy[12] notes there are numerous advantages for drill work by way of the computer. They are infinitely patient and allow students to take their time, providing as much practice as the students need. There is little ego involvement on the part of students, since their mistakes are not seen by their classmates or the instructor. The best drill programs have instructional value and possess a computer management system that allows the teacher to review how well each student did on tasks assigned. Those that are best for extending reading interests have fascinating game-like activities and show interest-arousing graphics.

Computer Simulations

If secondary instructors are to promote reading interests, they must project the concept that reading is an active process and the reader must have some purpose for reading. Unfortunately, this is where much traditional instruction in reading comprehension breaks down. The reader's own motivation or needs guide reading progress. It therefore makes sense to teach reading comprehension in a context that provides the reader with a sense of purpose for interacting with the text. Computer simulations can provide this by requiring readers to interact with text in order to accomplish some purpose.[13]

There are a number of advantages for promoting simulated computer activities for secondary students who are intent upon building an extended level of reading interest and skill development. *First,* the activities provide for variety and a high level of anticipation as the reader makes choices and receives immediate feedback. The simulations demand the careful attention of the learners and reward them if they make the correct choices. *Second,* the role of the reader is changed from a passive stance to one that is active, since an immediate response is demanded for most simulating activities. *Third,* most secondary students develop a purpose for reading and like to pursue worthwhile goals such as improving comprehension or reading speed.

Selecting Computer Software

Since there are literally hundreds of different kinds of software available for helping secondary readers, instructors and administrators should exercise judgment and evaluate the materials about to be purchased. The following are questions that should be answered.

1. **Is there any kind of warranty available by the seller?** Since many types of discs are subject to defect, this is an important consideration. Many companies sell their products on an "as-is" basis.

2. **Is it possible to use only a part of the program without using the total program?** Sometimes an instructor needs only a segment of a program to help a certain student with a definitive skill. Information concerning this aspect should be obtained previous to the purchase of any software.

3. **Does the program make provision for a management or record-keeping system?** The availability of printed records of the strengths and limitations of individual students provides a convenient and authoritative source of data for parent-teacher conferences or for use by the school counselor.

4. **Is the program easy to use and "computer-friendly"?** Since students (as well as teachers) have varying levels of computer competence, the instructions should appear in clear *direct* fashion on the computer screen and in the operations manual. A careful review of this important aspect *before* purchasing the software is vital.

5. **Is the reading difficulty level of the lessons appropriate for the secondary students who will be using them?** In every case they should be at the instructional reading level of the user. For some students who are especially problem readers, the reading level should be at the independent level. (Instructional level is the reading level where the student can demonstrate at least 75 percent comprehension when reading silently. Independent level is where 90 percent comprehension is obtained.)

6. **Are the graphics utilized with the program direct, appropriate, and closely correlated with the text?** Unfortunately, some graphics tend to distract the user and constitute a significant hindrance. Generally, secondary students require fewer graphics than is the case with elementary learners.

7. **Is there definitive evidence that the program content is accurate and well**

constructed? It should be completely free of any grammatical or spelling errors, and the lessons should be innovative and interesting, taking full advantage of sound, color, and extension activities.

8. **Does the program offer an instructional guide for the instructor?** The guides or packages should include an assortment of helpful data pieces that include teacher directions, complete analyses of program content and learning goals, the age and grade level for which it was designed, supplementary enrichment exercises, and recommendations for related lessons.

9. **Can the program be utilized by more than one student?** Programs with high utility can be employed for both small and large group structures.

10. **Has an investigation been conducted regarding recent reviews of the program?** There are numerous professional journals that publish reviews of all types of programs. Some of these publications include the *Journal of Courseware Review, Classroom Computer News,* and *Computer Teacher.*

Computers can serve an important function for supplying enrichment activities for students who desire to build lifelong reading interests. If programs are chosen wisely, they can provide variety and interesting branching possibilities.

SUMMARY

In order to build the level of reading interest for secondary students, it is important to undertake an evaluation process to determine their present reading interests. The reading interest and reading attitudes inventory included in this chapter should be very useful.

Learners must receive sufficient motivation before they can realize successful results in building reading interest. A number of principles should be followed if such a program is to achieve results. Various teaching strategies may be used in all content areas to improve motivation.

Computer-assisted instruction may be used by employing drill-and-practice lessons, word processing procedures, and computer simulations. All programs selected should be evaluated carefully before they are purchased and utilized with students.

REFERENCES

1. Karlin, Robert. *Teaching Reading in High School* (Fourth Edition). New York, Harper and Row, 1984, p. 318.

2. Burmeister, Lou E. *Reading Strategies for Middle and Secondary School Teachers* (Second Edition). Reading, Massachusetts, Addison-Wesley Publishing Company, 1978, p. 69.

3. E. B. Page, "Teacher Comments and Student Performance," *Studies in Educational Psychology*, (Raymond G. Kuhlen, Editor). Waltham, Massachusetts, Blaisdell Publishing Co., 1968, p. 270.

4. Claunch, Beverly and Patricia Nutt, "Nonreaders Are Made, Not Born: 16 Ways to Turn Off a Reader." *English Journal*, V. 76, N. 1 (January, 1987), p. 84.

5. Zintz, Miles V. and Zelda R. Maggart. *Corrective Reading* (Fifth Edition). Dubuque, Iowa, Wm. C. Brown, 1986, pp. 334–335.

6. Alexander, J. Estill (General Editor). *Teaching Reading* (Second Edition). Boston, Little Brown, 1983, p. 376.

7. Cushenbery, Donald C. *Improving Reading Skills in the Content Area.* Springfield, Charles C Thomas, Publisher, 1985, pp. 102–103.

8. Early, Margaret. *Reading to Learn in Grades 5 to 12.* New York, Harcourt Brace Jovanovich, 1984, pp. 266–267.

9. Smith, Harriett, "A Quick Fix for Agitata." *Journal of Reading,* V. 30, N. 8 (May, 1987), p. 726.

10. Roe, Betty D., Barbara D. Stoodt, and Paul C. Burns. *Secondary School Reading Instruction, the Content Areas.* Boston, Houghton Mifflin, 1987, p. 424.

11. Kinzer, Charles K., "A 5-Part Categorization for Use of Microcomputers in Reading Classrooms." *Journal of Reading,* V. 30, N. 3 (December, 1986), p. 226.

12. Balajthy, Ernest, "Reinforcement and Drill by Microcomputer." *The Reading Teacher,* V. 37, N. 6 (February, 1984), pp. 490–494.

13. Brady, Philip, "Computer Simulations and Reading Instruction." *The Computing Teacher,* V. 14, N. 2 (October, 1986), p. 34.

Chapter VII

BUILDING EXEMPLARY
SECONDARY READING PROGRAMS

Since the beginning of the construction of the American educational system, there has been much emphasis placed on the development of basic reading skills for *elementary* pupils. In the late 1800s and the early 1900s few students completed high school; therefore, it was necessary for reading proficiency to be built during the younger years while the students were involved in the process of schooling. Only during the past two or three decades has much attention been given to the construction of organized developmental, remedial, and corrective reading programs for secondary students. The younger members of a current faculty may remember reading classes in seventh and eighth grades but not in high school. Most high school programs have targeted on some remedial and speed-reading classes; however, few teachers can remember their content teachers teaching them how to read and study. Their memories consist of teachers who assigned and corrected, asked questions and evaluated answers, but seldom were there any lessons dealing with reading and studying.[1]

The lack of a long-term, established *secondary* reading program in many school systems may be partially responsible for the high rate of functional illiteracy that appears to abound in the United States. Some authorities believe that as many as one in five adults may be functionally incompetent because of their inability to answer simple questions relating to well-established data surrounding such areas as consumer economics and law. Unfortunately, many students fail to complete a total high school program, because they have become discouraged with their progress in reading and feel they have only one alternative left to them and that is to join the ranks of the "dropouts."

Secondary principals and classroom teachers now recognize that reading development is a total commitment and involves *all* students at the high school level. A developmental program must be an established,

128

ongoing curriculum to extend the reading competencies of the average reader. Enrichment opportunities must be provided for able readers, while precise remedial activities must be available for problem readers. There should be numerous provisions within the curriculum for each learner to proceed at his or her maximum level of achievement in reading.

In Chapter I, numerous characteristics of a useful secondary reading program were listed along with the role of the secondary teacher in implementing such a program. These were data relating to an *overall* program of instruction, whereas the purposes of this chapter are to provide precise information regarding the philosophical constructs and details surrounding precise identifiable programs. Accordingly, the following two topics are discussed in this chapter: philosophy and goals of the secondary reading program and descriptions of current exemplary secondary reading programs. A summary and a body of references conclude the chapter.

PHILOSOPHY AND GOALS OF THE SECONDARY READING PROGRAM

If a secondary reading program is to function as a viable tool for enhancing reading development of all students, it should be surrounded by certain identifiable philosophical bases. Since the characteristics of such a program (with emphasis on daily practices) were discussed in Chapter I, the philosophy and administration guidelines discussed in this segment refer mostly to the areas of program philosophy and personnel needed to insure that the curriculum is functional and useful. The successful current programs described in the next segment rate well with respect to all of the segments in the areas of desired daily practices, philosophy and personnel.

Philosophy of the Program

The reading program developed for each school must be uniquely designed to meet the precise needs of the students enrolled in that school. In some schools a coordinating committee makes essential decisions regarding the overall philosophy and basic functions of the program. Some of the questions that need to be addressed are as follows:

a. What types and kinds of students will be served in the reading program?
b. Is there a sufficient budget to purchase the required materials, services, and tests that may be needed to maintain a first-class program?
c. How shall special classes be organized? Will there be remedial, college-bound, and/or speed-reading sections?
d. What kind of course credit, if any, will be allowed for special reading classes?
e. How will the secondary reading curriculum be coordinated with the elementary reading program in the system?
f. Who will be the overall reading coordinator and what will be his or her duties for the position?
g. What types of in-service training will be offered to teachers to help insure that all instructors have a responsibility for teaching basic reading skills in his or her content area?

The analysis of numerous curriculum materials published by various well-known school systems indicates that most of them have a basic core of fundamental segments that constitute their philosophical base. The following are descriptions of several elements.

1. **The overall skills and objectives designed for the secondary school should be a part of a well-developed sequential approach that continues in a logical manner.** Reading is not a subject in the strictest sense but rather a body of skills to be taught in all content areas. Reading growth is a lifelong process and much significant growth can and should take place during the secondary school years.

2. **All secondary teachers should understand that there is a close inter-relationship among the four language arts — reading, speaking, listening, and writing.** Reading skills must be instructed from the *whole language* approach. Students should be taught to *listen, read* silently with a purpose, *write* thoughtfully constructed essays and reports, and *speak* directly and coherently about the information that has been read or heard about. Meaningful practice should be given to allow learners to receive coordinated practice in all of these areas.

3. **The program must be guided toward the accomplishment of identifiable goals.** The school staff must know what their objectives are. They must

think about what they are to accomplish together as a team.[2]

4. Probably the most important of all philosophical goals is that of designing a program of instruction that will meet the exact needs of each learner. This concept requires that educators construct a well-designed plan of studies that includes evaluation of each learner's needs, a program of appropriate instruction to meet those needs, and an ongoing study to help determine if those goals are being met.

DESCRIPTIONS OF CURRENT EXEMPLARY SECONDARY READING PROGRAMS

Before adopting or adapting any program, various conditions must be present if complete success is to be realized. The following are three important aspects.

1. Reading specialists and trained teachers are available to give proper professional advice and direction while the program is constructed and during the time it is operational in the school. The specialist should serve as a resource person to the total staff in demonstrating teaching techniques, organizing and coordinating school reading committees, conducting in-service meetings, and producing staff and parent bulletins relating to present and future goals and plans of the administrative staff and faculty for developmental, remedial, and special reading programs. He or she may wish to provide supplementary training for teachers that will provide them with the necessary base of skills for developing and promoting various student reading competencies within their content classes. The success or failure of a given reading program or curriculum may well reside on the presence or absence of a competent, well-trained reading specialist. He or she should possess extensive graduate training at an accredited institution that has courses and clinics that conform to the recommended standards for the training of reading specialists as recommended by the International Reading Association.

The following is a description of the course requirement guidelines for reading specialists as developed by the Professional Standards and Ethics Committee of the International Reading Association.*

---

*A copy of the complete standards can be obtained by writing to the International Reading Association, 800 Barksdale Road, P.O. Box 8139, Newark, Delaware 19714-8139.

CATEGORY II: READING SPECIALISTS (Roles 3,4,5,6)[3]

The preparation of Diagnostic-Remedial Specialists (Role 3), Developmental Reading-Study Skills Specialists (Role 4), Reading Consultant/ Reading Resource Teacher (Role 5) requires a minimum of 18–24 graduate credit hours in reading education courses from among:

Language Arts
Content Area Reading, Study, and Thinking Skills
Evaluation of Reading and Related Abilities
Children's or Adolescent Literature
Psychology of Reading
Sociology of Reading
Assessment of Reading Difficulties
Correction of Reading and Related Deficiencies
Clinical Practicum Internship
Seminar in Reading Research
College and Adult Reading Programs
Reading and the Learning Disabled Student
Teaching English As a Second Language

The preparation of Reading Coordinator/Supervisor (Role 6) should be three to six credit hours in supervision and administration courses and an additional three to six credit hours in specialized reading courses from among:

Action Research and Program Evaluation in Reading
Supervision and Organization of Reading Programs
Internship in Clinical or Field Based Supervision

2. Identifiable, sufficient funds are available for the possible employment of one or more reading specialists and the purchases of necessary instructional materials. As noted in this volume, there are many new, innovative media materials and computer software that are available to school authorities. While each item has value for certain students, a careful evaluative process must be undertaken for the selective purchase of adequate materials. For example, school officials may want to purchase a large number of high interest-low vocabulary books for reluctant readers and selected computer software for gifted and talented learners.

Even though commercial materials are essential to the development of any viable program, an adequate amount of money should be made available for those reading specialists and content teachers who desire to construct and duplicate teacher-made activities. A special budget amount may be established for the assessment and evaluation phases of the curriculum. Included in this category would be commercial tests and computer software evaluation devices.

3. **The program adopted is usable, practical, and based on the needs of the students for whom it is intended.** While there are many worthwhile, innovative programs currently functioning, a careful analysis of each segment should be undertaken to see if they can be transported to a different school location. The final adoption of a program should not be undertaken until a very carefully designed needs assessment has been undertaken, necessary funds are provided, and appropriate, professional guidance is available.

4. **A continuous program of informal evaluation is in evidence.** There are numerous questions that may be asked to judge the value of a secondary reading program. Wood[4] suggests many questions that may be asked. Items such as the following can be utilized:

   a. Do teachers take the responsibility of meeting student needs seriously?
   b. Do instructors know their materials so they can offer valid options to the students?
   c. Is the school a non-threatening, caring place where a student can safely expose his or her limitations and expect help?
   d. Is the school well equipped with multilevel materials, K–12, providing something for everyone, either remedial or enrichment?
   e. Do the physical facilities contribute to the learning process? Is there comfortable heat, light, ventilation, and a pleasing room arrangement?
   f. Do parents notice marked improvement in their students' reading behavior and attitudes?
   g. Do counselors and teachers find the students with limited reading ability becoming more open in asking for help and in taking reading risks?

5. **The secondary reading program should be a logical extension of a well-devised elementary and middle school reading program.** Nicholas Criscuolo[5] notes that regular academic classes should provide advanced reading skills for all secondary students. The best results come from a carefully articulated K–12 reading program in which a list of reading skills is distributed each year to content area teachers, along with suggested strategies for incorporating these skills into their respective disciplines. In such a program, all teachers are reading teachers, especially when they teach study skills, vocabulary development, reading for main idea or sequence, and reference techniques.

Program Descriptions

Included in this section are descriptions of various selected secondary reading programs in the United States. Some of them are included in *Educational Programs That Work* (13th Ed.) published in 1987. The publication can be obtained by writing to SOPHIS WEST, INC., 1120 Delaware Avenue, Longmont, Colorado 80501. (Program titles designated with the letters (EPTW) are included in this publication.) Others have been recommended to the author by area and regional reading authorities. A short description of each program is provided along with the name of the school official to consult for more detailed information. Many features of the programs can be easily transported to other schools with much success. Appreciation is extended to the listed project directors for permission given to the author to include an edited description of their program in this volume.

APPENDICES

Appendix A

ALBUQUERQUE, NEW MEXICO
MIDDLE SCHOOL READING PROGRAM

Albuquerque Public Schools
725 University, S.E.
P.O. Box 25704
Albuquerque, New Mexico 87125

Ellen D. Foster, Language Arts/Reading Coordinator
Anne C. Tarleton, Reading Specialist

The Middle School Reading Program provides the last formal reading instruction for all students in the Albuquerque Public Schools. This is accomplished in the Middle School Language/Literature or Literature classes. Reading skills are also taught in all content area classes as these instructors use reading skills necessary for learning in their content areas. To insure lifelong personal reading development, reading for pleasure and reading for information are also emphasized through the formal and content area reading programs.

The goals of the reading program in the middle school as students and teachers become actively involved in the reading process are the following:

1. Developing sequential skills in vocabulary and comprehension
2. Meeting individual needs through reteaching and enrichment activities
3. Analyzing and enjoying literature
4. Developing higher level thinking skills
5. Refining strategies in content reading and composition
6. Preparing for the future with study skills, life skills, and career skills
7. Testing to evaluate the reading program and provide diagnostic information

The Language and Literature courses are organized in several different ways:

- Language/Literature blocks lasting two or three periods are required of each student in school
- Separate Language Arts and Literature (Reading) classes
- Language/Literature classes required at sixth grade level and language arts classes required at seventh and eighth grade levels
- Language/Literature classes may be offered as electives at seventh and eighth grades.

The individual middle school determines specific course content, length of instructional periods, and course requirements for students.

137

ALBUQUERQUE, NEW MEXICO
SECONDARY READING PROGRAM

Albuquerque Public Schools
725 University, S.E.
P.O. Box 25704
Albuquerque, New Mexico 87125

Ellen D. Foster, Language Arts/Reading Coordinator
Anne C. Tarleton, Reading Specialist

The goal of the *Albuquerque Public Schools Secondary Reading Program* is to develop an awareness of the student's needs and the teacher's role in meeting those needs. This goal is accomplished through a reading program concentrating on three major phases:

DEVELOPMENTAL—"Learning to Read"
   Developing skills which allow students to learn to read to the best of their ability in each content area
FUNCTIONAL—"Reading to Learn"
   Promoting functional use of reading in order to foster learning
RECREATIONAL—"Liking to Read"
   Establishing a sense of the informational and recreational uses of reading

The program is flexible in its approach to the various content areas, and dependent upon the combined efforts of the principals, administrators, teachers, support staff, reading teacher/consultants, parents and students. A handbook is made available to all content area teachers which provides specific information about teaching reading skills to older students. The major sections of the book contain explanations of the components of the secondary reading program and help to facilitate instruction for those teachers who wish to add to their repertoire of strategies and techniques.

The district realizes that teachers, like students, are at different stages of growth and development; therefore, information needed by one teacher may be of limited interest or use to another. The handbook is organized as a teaching tool so that teachers may seek out areas of interest according to their needs. The handbook and the availability of the reading teacher/consultants provide teachers with unlimited resources for implementation of the secondary reading program. It includes such things as information about (1) the role of secondary reading teacher/consultants and how they can be of help to content area teachers, (2) New Mexico Language Arts Reading Competencies from third to eighth grades, and (3) teacher and principal guides for implementing the reading program. There is also an evaluation for reading instruction, covering responsibilities of teachers, principals, librarians, supervisors, and parents.

A special section on "Teaching Reading in Content Areas" includes all areas of the curriculum from business, education and physical education to foreign languages and mathematics. Other sections are on diagnosis, comprehension, readability, vocabulary skills, study skills, and reading for pleasure.

Appendix C

BAKERSFIELD, CALIFORNIA DEMONSTRATION PROGRAM IN ENGLISH/LANGUAGE ARTS (EPTW)

CALIFORNIA DEMONSTRATION PROGRAM
English/Language Arts
Sierra Junior High School
3017 Center Street
Bakersfield, California 93306
Elizabeth McCray, Project Director
(805) 323-4838

The CALIFORNIA DEMONSTRATION PROGRAM in English/language arts serves an important role in developing the ability of all students to communicate in the English language and use critical thinking skills.

Students gain English language proficiencies by reading a central core of literary works that focuses on the significant issues of human civilization. The skills of reading, writing, listening, and speaking are developed in a systematic study of these works. Students actively use their language arts skills to comprehend and develop the ideas and values that these works embody.

All students are serviced, including limited-English-proficient students, educationally disadvantaged students, those students achieving at a level significantly below their peers, gifted and talented students, and students receiving special education instruction and services. Students are heterogeneously grouped for instructional periods of 50 minutes.

The English/language arts curriculum is comprehensive, systematic, and developmental. The curriculum is organized around a central core of literary works selected by the district from among the great essays, poems, short stories, novels, biographies, dramas, folktales, and speeches that preserve and embody the diverse cultural heritage of the United States. English teachers use literature both

(1) as the medium for teaching the fundamental human, ethical, cultural, and political values that underlie our society and connect us as human beings and
(2) as the means for teaching reading, writing, listening, speaking, and thinking skills at all grade levels.

The curriculum is developmentally sequenced so that all students gain an increased understanding of the works of literature that are studied and thus are better prepared to read and comprehend similar works on their own.

140

THE LITERATURE CURRICULUM

A core program consisting of those works that are intensely studied and discussed on a classwide basis.

An extended program consisting of similar works selected by students with the teacher's guidance.

A recreational/motivational reading program to develop the reading habits of students and to instill in them the lifelong pleasures and rewards of reading.

OTHER COMPONENTS

Students receive instruction and assistance in library and media use and how to access and use a range of information sources. Libraries are open before and after school to encourage the maturation of students as independent learners. Libraries also offer support services for teachers by helping them integrate library use in regular assignments.

Computers fulfill a variety of functions. Word processing programs support and extend the writing component of the curriculum, and students have an opportunity to become familiar with many types of computers. Composition and editing skills are enhanced by the word processing programs, since computers are good motivators for students as they use printouts.

One goal of the Demonstration Program is to have each student write, print, and bind his or her own book. Students are encouraged to enter their books in the Young Author Fair organized by the local reading association.

CINCINNATI, OHIO SCHWAB MIDDLE SCHOOL READING PROGRAM

SCHWAB MIDDLE SCHOOL

Cincinnati, Ohio
Dr. Alfred Ciana
Ms. Kelley Loetscher
University of Cincinnati
608 Teachers College Building
Cincinnati, Ohio 45221-0002

The Schwab Middle School is an urban school in Cincinnati, Ohio with students in grades seven and eight. The school is at the 65-percent poverty level and is located in a working-class neighborhood. It is an alternative school for the Advanced College Preparatory Program of the Cincinnati Public Schools, and draws students from all areas of the city.

The approach to this program is the linking of reading and writing or a whole language, student-centered, process approach. It involves the commitment of a teacher to working with learners both in and out of the classroom, becoming part of their community, and involving parents in the learning process. It is based upon Nancie Atwell's book, *In The Middle*, in which she describes an immersion approach to reading and writing in the middle school.

The school day in the Schwab Middle School is organized around seven 40-minute class periods, with language arts and reading grouped into double periods. Since it is imperative that a community be established at the beginning of the school year, classroom teachers first telephone or visit the parent or legal guardian of every student enrolled in their classes. In these initial interviews, they stress the importance of communication and keeping in contact with the school, as well as having high expectations for the students. In addition, they explain the homework policy of having reading and writing done at home and monitored by the parent or other appropriate adult. Parents and students are encouraged to participate in this way for at least one hour per day, including weekends. They are given a checklist and asked to keep track of the length of time spent on reading and writing at home and rate their children each night as doing excellent, average, or poor. The student then brings this report to school at the end of every two weeks to be recorded by the teacher.

The establishment of a community of language learners is begun the first day of school when the students are given a letter that explains the language arts process program. The first segment of the block of time is for Writing and the second is for

142

Reading. There are strict rules of participation, following the suggestions of Nancie Atwell.

The writing period begins each day with a "free write," during which time students write and share something from their notebooks. Next, there is a mini-lesson of five to seven minutes that briefly addresses some aspect of language which needs to be taught or reinforced. The remaining twenty-five minutes are spent on writing workshop with students developing a piece for evaluation. Three pieces are required each quarter and must be accompanied by two rough drafts. While the students are writing, the teacher circulates around the room and does a "Status of the Class." This serves to keep a running account of what each student does daily and is on the basis for future lesson plans regarding some aspect of language identified as a problem. During this time students may sign up for a teacher conference.

After a four-minute class break, students are to be in their seats with a book of their choosing. To facilitate this, the first Thursday of each month the librarian from the neighborhood branch of the public library sends a collection of 100 books to the school on a variety of subjects. The reading class begins either with a mini-lesson or a "read-aloud." Mini-lessons typically address some aspect or element of literature (characterization, plot, setting, etc.) or may deal with one author or a collected set of the author's works. For the read-aloud, the teacher reads to the class ten minutes. In the remaining thirty minutes, students participate in silent reading of their library books.

One last activity for students is to make an entry in their literature logs. In this they must write about some aspect of their book they would like to think further about. The entry is addressed to the teacher and he/she responds with further comments for the student to think about. In their entries, students may tell what they liked about the book, what they thought or felt and why, what the book meant personally, why it was selected, and ask questions of the teacher.

Evaluation for the course is done throughout the semester, with free writing assessed weekly. During individual conferences, goals are outlined and evaluated. A process exam is given at the end of the grading period in which students must develop a piece as they would for the selected writing, that is, two drafts with a final piece. Materials needed for this program are minimal and include a notebook for each class, a pen or pencil, and trade books which can be purchased or provided. Administrative support is not only critical but imperative. Teachers must be made to feel confident that the changes taking place in students' reading/writing skills are worthwhile and effective.

COEUR D'ALENE, IDAHO PUBLIC SCHOOLS
READ:S PROGRAM (EPTW)

Coeur d'Alene Public Schools
311 N. 10th Street
Coeur d'Alene, Idaho 83814
Lynn Dennis, Director
Project READ:S
(208) 664-8241

Project READ:S is a nationally validated reading-in-the-content-area program that has been adopted and adapted by hundreds of teachers, schools, and school districts throughout the nation. The purpose of Project READ:S is to provide content area teachers with the skills to develop instructional modules in vocabulary, comprehension, and study skills using the content of their current courses. These modules offer students reinforcement through guided and individual practice of the reading skills taught in the students' English and/or reading classes.

What is especially attractive to content area teachers is that they are not asked to become reading teachers. Project READ:S provides teachers of any subject area with already developed lesson-design formats based upon an adopted hierarchy of reading skills being taught directly in the reading/English classrooms. By incorporating the reading process in the content of any subject matter, teachers are providing their students with daily opportunities to practice reading skills already taught in English/reading while mastering the content of history, science, math, foreign language, art, welding, music, P.E., or any other subject area. Also, teachers work together on mutually taught text-units and are able to share inghts into problems and gain an enhanced understanding of their subject and how best to teach it. The underlying philosophy of the teaching process of READ:S is the Madeline Hunter Essential Elements of Instruction model that is a top teacher priority in-service program for most school districts across the nation. Project READ:S is also used by districts to infuse critical thinking skills into all subject areas.

Project READ:S—Reading Education Accountability Design: Secondary is approved for grades 7–12 and is affiliated with the U.S. Department of Education's National Diffusion Network Program. It is a low-cost, proven means of teaching measurable, adult-level reading skills to junior and senior high school students as an integral part of all their content area subjects. It addresses the two critical goals of reading ability and content mastery in upper-grade levels and is adaptable to any population of American students.

The approach provides a teacher-based in-service component that builds teacher confidence and allows teachers to use their own lesson plans in presenting content area material to students. In Project READ:S teachers learn how to reinforce a hierarchy of 60 essential reading skills that are the foundation of the students' instruction in their language arts/English/reading classes. It is the cumulative effect on students of constantly being required in each academic discipline to utilize their attained reading skills that is the central thrust of Project READ:S.

CRANSTON, RHODE ISLAND
COMPREHENSIVE READING PROGRAM (EPTW)

CRANSTON'S COMPREHENSIVE READING PROGRAM
Department of Reading Services
845 Park Avenue
Cranston, Rhode Island 02910
Roberta A. Costa
Project Coordinator
(401) 785-0400, Ext. 285

The philosophy of Cranston's Comprehensive Reading Program is that reading is a thinking process involving meaningful interaction between the reader and written language. Learning to read is considered to be developmental in nature and, as such, is part of the broad spectrum of skills that incorporates listening, speaking, and writing. An important premise of the program is that each student needs to acquire skills, have opportunities to apply skills in content area subjects and real-life situations, and come to appreciate reading as a pleasurable leisure-time pursuit. The quality of instruction determines the extent to which these needs are met.

The major objectives of the reading program, both elementary and secondary, are the following:

1. To provide a developmental reading program that meets the needs of the below average, average, and above average student.
2. To provide an adequate readiness program that will include the necessary pre-reading skills for successful entry into a reading program.
3. To provide the student with a reading program that will teach him to decode words and their meanings, and to operate at the cognitive levels of reading comprehension—literal, interpretive, analytical, critical, and creative.
4. To develop the student's ability to transfer his decoding and comprehension skills, in the application of these skills, to content area subjects.
5. To develop student's ability to become an independent learner by developing learning/study skills in content area subjects.
6. To develop students who view reading as an enjoyable experience and who use their reading skills for recreational reading.
7. To provide a support system for students and staff, through the use of reading specialists, to assist in the ongoing improvement of student performance and the overall quality of the reading program.

146

CCRP addresses the varied reading needs of secondary school students. For those students who still need additional time to master basic reading skills, a reading guide, *Intensified Reading Skills Program,* serves to define and guide the program. This is used by reading specialists and content area teachers to provide instruction in core reading skills.

For those students who have mastered the basic reading skills, the ongoing development of higher order skills is incorporated into content area instruction. The *Content Area Strategies Handbook* was developed by secondary school teachers and reading specialists for use in English, math, social studies and science classes. This book helps the content area teacher with instructional strategies for integrating the learning/study skills into content subject material. The teacher's handbook contains model lessons by content area that demonstrate how learning/study skills can be integrated into content material. Background information and the rationale for inclusion of study skills into various curricula is also provided. A student handbook, *Breakthrough,* provides an introduction to basic study skills and serves as an ongoing reference. Another booklet, the *Secondary Teachers' Handbook for the Improvement of Reading in Every Classroom* provides a comprehensive in-depth introduction to reading instruction, selection of appropriate textbooks, material, informal evaluation measures, readability formulae, and reading skills lists specific to each content area.

Staff development activities including in-service courses, summer workshops, and departmental meetings have become the vehicle for reconceptualizing and designing Cranston's learning/study skills program. Each secondary school has the responsibility to design an implementation plan, focusing on the specific needs of their staff and students.

Appendix G

DEXTER, NEW MEXICO JR. HIGH
READING PROGRAM

Dexter Consolidated Schools
Dexter, New Mexico 88230
Patricia C. Irwin, Director of Reading

This reading program serves the entire seventh and eighth grade student body in a small school district. Classes meet daily for 45 to 50 minutes. The program includes individualized instruction, large and small group work, reading aloud, sustained silent reading, and a reading/writing connection.

Individualized instruction is based on the results of the criterion-referenced PRI Test (CTB/McGraw) which is given as a pre- and post-test. Skills assignments are keyed to a wide variety of commercially produced materials. Students are given contracts of from two to three weeks in length and the assignments on these are graded by the students. Mastery tests are given after practice on needed skills. This skills work is done three days a week for 20 to 25 minutes each day.

Group work includes such activities as perception exercises and puzzles, logic puzzles, brainstorming, role playing, word games, cooperative writing, holiday activities, newspaper scavenger hunts, and many others.

The teacher reads aloud to each class every day. Books used have included *The Pinballs* by Betsy Byars, *The Lion, the Witch, and The Wardrobe* by C.S. Lewis, *Summer of the Monkeys* by Wilson Rawls, *Stranger With My Face* by Lois Duncan, and *Dear Mr. Henshaw* by Beverly Cleary.

Sustained Silent Reading is included in the curriculum three days a week for a period of ten minutes each day. Students have access to a variety of books as well as donated magazines and newspapers. During this period, student/teacher conferences are held to discuss progress and to draw up new contracts.

The reading/writing connection assignment involves reading a novel of the student's choice for from 25 to 30 minutes, then writing a brief summary, questions about the reading, and a prediction. This writing is graded by the teacher.

The program is now entering its third year and is deemed a success based upon increased test scores and student enjoyment of all types of reading material as determined by student surveys.

Appendix H

DUBLIN, OHIO
MIDDLE SCHOOL READING PROGRAM

Dublin Middle School
150 West Bridge Street
Dublin, Ohio 43017
(614) 764-5919
(Donna Patterson, District Reading Coordinator)

The Dublin Middle School consists of sixth, seventh, and eighth grades. The courses are two semesters each and are required courses. The objective for all three grades is to teach READING TO LEARN strategies and reinforce LEARNING TO READ skills. The focus lies in two areas:

1. Student habits and attitudes toward reading for pleasure and for information.
2. Student comprehension and retention of text.

Materials include both high interest paperback novels chosen by themes and the students' content area textbooks. Instructional approaches include the writing process, cooperative group learning or student-structured discussion, and content study strategies such as the development of leveled question and study skills strategies.

There are three components to the reading program: (1) reading real books, (2) using the writing process, and (3) learning study skills. An integrated approach is utilized in all the language arts—listening, speaking, reading, and writing. During each grading period, students are introduced to several themes and asked to select books to read. Book lists are provided for each grade and these are used each night in homework assignments. In addition to classroom lessons, each student is asked to complete some type of project, artistic writing, or drama which reflects his/her individual response to the theme.

Appendix I

DUBLIN, OHIO
SECONDARY READING PROGRAM

Dublin High School
6780 Coffman Road
Dublin, Ohio 43017
(614) 764-5900
(Donna Patterson, District Reading Coordinator)

The philosophy for the reading program is based on whole language acquisition—that students LEARN TO READ in concert with learning to think, speak, and write. At the secondary level, the student READS TO LEARN. This requires practical strategies in order to gather, comprehend, and retain information.

Currently, four reading courses are offered: *High School Prep Reading* is a half-year, one credit, elective course for ninth and tenth grade students designed to help them meet the demands of high school reading. *College Prep Reading* is a half-year, one credit, elective course for eleventh and twelfth grade students to help them meet the demands of college reading. *Critical Reading* is a half-year, one credit, elective course for eleventh and twelfth grade students and is intended to train them to view a particular issue from various perspectives through text. *Individualized Reading* is a 9-week, ¼ credit, elective course offered to any student at the high school.

The overall purpose of the secondary reading program is to provide reading instruction in such a way that all students can acquire and maintain the reading skills necessary to achieve success in their educational pursuits. Planning, implementation, and evaluation is a cooperative effort involving the reading specialist, content area instructors, school administrators, support personnel, parents, and students. In-service education for the staff is included in the overall program.

Diagnosis: A sequential approach is used to identify the reading needs of individual students, with a criterion-referenced test being administered at the beginning of the school year to all entering students. Further diagnosis is used to identify the needs of students who are severely disabled and those with specific skill weaknesses.

Instructional Programs: The reading specialist is responsible for implementing a voluntary, individualized diagnostic, prescriptive reading center program. The reading center provides supplemental reading services, and does not replace any subject matter, class, or program. Content area instructors are key figures in identifying the skills needed by students, and cooperation with the reading specialist helps students expand their reading skill development. The total reading program is systematic, sequential, and continuous, and the students develop a growing awareness

150

of different purposes for reading. A major goal of the total school reading program is to improve student attitudes toward reading. Instruction is planned in a way that guarantees success and promotes positive reading attitudes.

Evaluation: Evaluation of the total reading program is a cooperative effort and includes information from students, administrators, content area instructors, support personnel, the reading specialist, and parents. Evaluation is an ongoing process.

EUCLID, OHIO
READING AND VOCABULARY FOR
THE COLLEGE BOUND

Euclid Public Schools
711 East 222nd Street
Euclid, Ohio 44123
Dolores J. Black, Reading Supervisor
(216) 261-2900 Ext. 306

Reading and Vocabulary for the College Bound

This is a one-semester course for junior and senior high students who want to become more efficient readers. It is recommended for students who have already mastered the basic reading skills necessary to read and comprehend college-level reading materials. The course emphasizes three higher-level reading and writing skills: critical reading and writing, vocabulary, and reading efficiency or speed.

The semester is divided into segments of study, beginning with the three levels of reading—literal, interpretive, and critical. Other areas of reading include instruction in skimming and scanning, organizational patterns, pacing, summaries, language style, synthesis, critical reading and thinking, logic, critique, advertisements, and propaganda. A SAT computer program is incorporated into the vocabulary study and many selected books and articles are used by the teaching staff. Some examples are *Be A Better Reader* by Nila Banton Smith, *Breaking the Reading Barrier* by D.W. Gilbert, and *Vocabulary for the College-Bound Student* by Harold Levine.

Each area of study includes reading and writing activities, vocabulary study, and speech activities. A student handbook is central to the course curriculum and includes the following:

I. Reading Improvement
   A. General purpose
   B. Specific purpose
   C. Attitude
II. Levels of Reading
   A. Literal
   B. Interpretive
   C. Critical

V. Propaganda Techniques
   A. Definition
   B. Use of
   C. Techniques
IV. Critical Reading
   A. How to
   B. Questions

III. Tone
    A. Kind
    B. How revealed

IV. Judgments
    A. Fact and opinion
    B. Quotes
    C. Authority
    D. Dates
    E. Begging the question
    F. Conclusions

VII. Improving Speed
    A. Kinds of readers
    B. Speed hinderers
    C. Overcoming problems

Appendix K

KALISPELL, MONTANA
CONTENT READING INCLUDING
STUDY SYSTEMS PROJECT (EPTW)

CRISS Project
233 First Avenue East
Kalispell, Montana 59901
(406) 755-5015
Ms. Lynn Havens, Director

The Content Reading (CRISS) Project is a staff development program for teachers in content areas, including study systems designed to teach students how to learn from textbook material. Its goal is to provide students with skills that will help them better organize, understand, and retain course information. The project presents the theoretical framework and guided practice in nine instructional strategies in a two- or three-day in-service. Teachers leave the workshop with the procedures and materials for immediate program implementation. All instructional materials are provided by the project. Participants are expected to purchase a manual which outlines the instructional strategies utilizing specific subject examples. Each topic is discussed in detail, and only this guide and the teachers' own texts are needed for the training.

INSTRUCTIONAL STRATEGIES

1. A review of the theory and how it relates to the strategies
2. Text Assessment
3. Student Assessment
4. Teaching Text Organization
5. Main Idea Development
6. Learning and Study Guides
7. Writing Activities
8. Vocabulary
9. Directed Reading Activity (DRA)

EVALUATION

An evaluation component is available through the CRISS project which is useful in assessing the program and students. These include an implementation checklist for teachers and pre- and post-tests for students.

THEORETICAL BASE

CRISS developers drew from cognitive psychology and reading research to create a base for the program. There are three key concepts: students must be able to integrate new information with prior knowledge; they must be actively involved in their own learning; and students must be able to monitor their own learning. Students are taught a wide variety of strategies for their learning style and reading purpose. In presenting CRISS strategies in the classroom, teachers use a direct instructional style which follows four sequential steps—introduction, modeling, guided practice, and independent application. These steps are followed throughout the CRISS program.

MINNEAPOLIS, MINNESOTA
READING POWER IN THE
CONTENT AREAS READING PROGRAM (EPTW)

READING POWER IN THE CONTENT AREAS
110 Pattee Hall
150 Pillsbury Drive S.E.
University of Minnesota
Minneapolis, MN 55455
Carol Burgess, Director
(612) 624-0067

The READING POWER project is a staff development program designed to increase *content area* teachers' awareness of the potential problems that may occur when there is a gap between student reading abilities and the reading requirements of content-specific printed instructional materials. The program provides those instructors with strategies designed to minimize the effects of this gap. The READING POWER project has been implemented in both academic and vocational schools across the nation.

The goals of the project:

- To narrow the gap between student reading ability and the skill level required to read printed instructional materials.
- To enrich content area teachers' knowledge, attitudes, and skills as they relate to the use of textbooks and other reading-related activities.
- To increase student learning of content while improving reading comprehension and thinking skills.

FIVE COMPONENTS ARE INCORPORATED TO ASSIST EVERY TEACHER WITH READING WITHIN THEIR CONTENT AREA. They are:

1. Material Assessment—Apply computerized or manual techniques to analyze the reading level of printed material and to modify teaching strategies to minimize the effect of differences between student reading ability and reading requirements of the materials.
2. Student Assessment—Train instructors to determine the reading abilities of their students through the use of standardized and teacher-developed tests.
3. Instructor Assessment—Assess teachers' knowledge and attitudes in the

selection and utilization of instructional material in their classrooms through the use of the Reading Power Survey and Teacher Inventory.

4. Instructional Strategies — Assist instructors to develop teaching strategies designed to increase students' general reading comprehension, knowledge of content-specific vocabulary, and content learning.

5. Ongoing In-Service — Provide assistance through follow-up training in project components including vocabulary, comprehension, and study skills and other selected topics.

INTENDED OUTCOMES OF THE READING POWER PROJECT

The READING POWER project consists of teacher-oriented activities designed to promote student reading improvement through change in both teacher and student behaviors.

Anticipated teacher outcomes include:

- The ability to better plan for instructional effectiveness.
- More satisfaction in student performance levels.
- A better student/teacher relationship.

Anticipated student outcomes:

- Increased ability to use content area materials more effectively for increased learning of content.
- Increased skill levels in vocabulary, reading comprehension, critical thinking skills, and self-directed learning.

The READING POWER project is *not* a "pull-out" remedial reading or isolated study skills program and should not be implemented as a replacement for these services. The project is designed to work in tandem with these programs to complement them and provide for the total integration of reading skills within content instruction.

Appendix M

MOUNT VERNON, OHIO
MIDDLE SCHOOL READING PROGRAM

MOUNT VERNON MIDDLE SCHOOL
Mt. Vernon City Schools
105 East Chestnut Street
Mount Vernon, Ohio 43050
Lori Beach
Marcia P. Orsborn, Reading Consultants

The eighth grade "Choices" reading program at the Mount Vernon Middle School has been met with much positive reaction from the students and staff. This program enables the students to choose reading classes for four of the six six-week units during the year. This has increased student motivation, as well as allowing teachers some choice as to the units they will teach.

Using the newly adopted textbook for eighth grade reading and literature, as well as supplemental resources, ten units of study were created, two of which would be required of all students. The eight remaining courses comprise the "Choices" program. On the first day of school, students are given a brief written description of the units and are asked to choose which they would like to study. To insure that results are based solely on interest, teacher assignments are not revealed and students are unaware of other's decisions.

During the first six weeks of the school year a required unit entitled "Don't Be Nutty, Study!" is taught. The use of SQ3R, making a study schedule and tips on how to improve the use of one's time, thus producing better grades, is featured. Other techniques to help with content area reading are also taught.

The first "choice" is experienced during the second six-weeks' time period. Students participate in "Who Wrote That?" or "Books R Us." "Who Wrote That?" is a study of authors popular to the Middle School age group (e.g. S.E. Hinton, Paula Danzinger, Madeleine L'Engle, Norma Fox Mazer). After an introduction to each author, students select one author to study in-depth. They read two to three of his/her books and write a research paper about the author. In "Books R Us," students explore various genre and the elements of fiction. They keep Response Journals to document and discuss their personal reading. They also give book talks and create project extensions of the novels read, and make paper and ink.

Thinking in a variety of ways is the theme of the third six-weeks, when students choose between "No Problem!" and "Frame It!" The first incorporates thinking skills, logic and problem-solving skills to find facts, generate ideas and look for

158

patterns. A study of inventions and inventors is also conducted. Independent and group projects include creating a variety of puzzles and inventions. "Frame It!" explores the art of visual thinking—cartooning. In this course, students interpret editorial cartoons as well as comic strips. They also learn the specialized vocabulary and symbols associated with cartooning. By the end of the six weeks, the students develop original cartoons or comic strips.

During the fourth six weeks, all students participate in a required course entitled "Careers." Through the use of an interest inventory, they each choose a career for which they may be well suited. Using the text, *Widening Pathways,* and a variety of library resources, they then do an in-depth exploration of that career, which results in a formal research paper. An on-site visitation day is included in this unit.

"As the Pages Turn" and "Back in Time" are the choices for the fifth six weeks. In "As the Pages Turn," students read a variety of short stories in which point of view, flashback, humor, and imagery are used. Besides using the reading text, they are permitted to bring examples of short stories from magazines, other texts, etc., to use for their independent study. "Back in Time" is a unit in which students read American historical fiction. Included in this study is colonizing America, the Revolutionary War, the Civil War, and the Depression. Independent reading and a final project covers other time periods, such as World War II or the sixties. Dramatizations and role playing are featured activities in this unit.

To conclude the school year, students have their final choice in either "In Search of . . ." or "Future Concerns." The first correlates with the eighth grade study of mental health in science, using the novels *Dicey's Song, A Ring of Endless Light,* and *Welcome Home, Jellybean.* Discussions about different problems relevant to teenagers and journal writing will also be a part of this course. "Future Concerns" is basically a science fiction study. Students read several fictional accounts of life in the future, participate in group projects dealing with scientific advancements, and research an independent topic. Novels for study include *Anna to the Infinite Power* and *The White Mountains.*

One challenge to the program is scheduling of teachers' classes in order for them to be able to "trade" students in a specific block of time. Another is evenly distributing students so that teachers have a proportionate number. When there is an overlarge student number for a unit, voluntary reassigning takes place.

Record keeping is done with grade sheets, folders, and anecdotal records, and this has proved workable, as one teacher is assigned certain students for the entire semester and is responsible for grades for the semester.

Appendix N

OMAHA, NEBRASKA
SECONDARY READING PROGRAMS

Omaha Public Schools
Reading Services Center
4215 South 20th Street
Omaha, Nebraska 68107

PURPOSES OF SECONDARY READING PROGRAMS
IN OMAHA

Two general purposes guide the use of reading curriculum:

1. To develop general reading skills commensurate with students' capabilities so they can function in life situations and read effectively for educational purposes and recreation.
2. To offer an instructional program that is efficient, follows the needs and interests of students, develops skills in areas representing community interests, covers skills recognized as important to effective reading ability, is consistent with sound principles in educational psychology, and follows a mastery learning design.

In these purposes one finds a special dedication to the learning of individual students. Remedial instruction programs are often a last ditch effort of the school to help the student develop reading and study skills consistent with the expectancy we have for high school graduates. Remedial reading instruction programs must be geared to continue each student's development of reading skills starting with his/her present skill and adding consistently to that skill. There is also a great interest here in efficiency. To catch up, the student must progress more quickly than other classmates. Instruction must be organized to produce the most skill for each student in the shortest period of time. This effort requires an optimistic expectancy of each student and a structured and efficient teaching process.

STUDENT CHARACTERISTICS

Students enrolled in Basic Skills and Developmental Reading classes bring a wide range of differences for the teacher to work with. It has been consistently true that reading classes show great diversity even though schools attempt to assign students selectively.

General Reading Ability

The first kind of diversity noted is usually the range of general reading ability. It is not unusual for students to vary in ability as many as five or six years in a single class. In one class analyzed it was judged that only about one-third of a selected class could profit from group assignments directed at students whose ability represented the average for the group.

Causation

The students also vary widely in the reason for their limited reading skills. Some are working against inherent limitations. Others are not motivated to learn. Some have language difficulties that affect reading. Many have not read enough at levels of difficulty where they can succeed in learning new vocabulary. The reading teacher is faced with all of these backgrounds and must organize instruction to improve the skills of each student.

Techniques of Reading

Then there is a more technical diversity found in the skill of students. Some have limited reading skill simply because they have not read enough. Some have such poor word-analysis skills that they are continually dependent on someone else to unlock new words; these students are not likely to improve their reading no matter how much they are assigned or encouraged to read independently. A variety of other technical problems also present themselves in each class of students.

It is clear that the diversity of student reading skill, background, and reading technique force a requirement for individual planning and instruction that is unusual in the secondary school tradition.

TECHNICAL INSTRUCTION IN READING

There is probably no subject of instruction which has been researched in greater depth than reading. There are specific methods that have been identified as efficient and productive. Selections of the "right" method is obviously dependent on the student who is being taught. This again poses two responsibilities for the teacher and school:

1. The teacher must be aware of the methods available.
2. The specific method that is most beneficial must be identified and offered to each student.

Since reading is focused on both skill and knowledge, there must be some assurance that the student receives enough guided practice in applying each developing skill so it becomes fluent and useful.

All of these technical considerations cry for ongoing contact of teachers with information about classroom organization, teaching methods, materials, diagnosis and learning psychology.

This need for interaction with sources of professional information suggest that the best reading program is staffed by a teacher who is in touch with other teachers, sources of research results, professional literature and effective practices. In turn, this requirement suggests that the best school or system reading program has support from a central office in curriculum development and teacher training. It also indicates the need for close communication among teachers to extend technical knowledge and problem-solving skills.

Prepared by:

Dr. Ronald Meyer, Supervisor of Special Projects
Mrs. Barbara Schweiger, Supervisor of Reading Services
Dr. Virginia Bryg, Reading Specialist
Ms. Kathleen Sullivan, Reading Specialist

Appendix O

ONTARIO–MONTCLAIR, CALIFORNIA
FUTUREPRINT JR. HIGH SCHOOL
READING PROGRAM (EPTW)

FUTUREPRINT
De Anza Junior High School
Ontario-Montclair School District
1450 South Sultana Avenue
Ontario, California 91761
Ann Glaser, Project Director
(714) 983-2118

FUTUREPRINT is a junior high school reading program that focuses on improving academic achievement and self-concept through: (a) accurately diagnosing the strengths and limitations of all incoming students; (b) tailoring personalized contracts to these assessments; (c) delivering consistent small group and individual instruction in a supportive learning environment using a variety of materials; and (d) providing timely feedback to students regarding both contract completion and test performance.

Goals and Objectives

FUTUREPRINT has two basic goals: to increase reading achievement and improve the self-concept of students so they will become more effective readers who will achieve academic success in high school. Two specific objectives are raising reading test scores and high school grade point averages.

In order to achieve these objectives, the FUTUREPRINT program provides intensive reading instruction that is diagnostic, prescriptive, and personalized, using a contract system in the supportive environment of a reading center. FUTUREPRINT offers two additional components: group counseling and the Preschool Story House.

Program Components

1. The program features the supportive environment of a reading center. This facility may be a library, a large classroom, or even part of a classroom.
2. Students are scheduled into the Reading Center in heterogeneous groups on a three-week rotation from a content class, receiving one-half year of the content class and one-half year of reading as well as a full year of

English. Other students are scheduled more frequently, according to their needs.

3. Diagnosis is the starting point. The student's strengths, needs, and interests are diagnosed, then a program of instruction is developed which conveys acceptance, develops responsibility, challenges expectations, and provides opportunities for growth.

4. A contract system is the heart of the program. Teachers write personalized contracts to guide their students' learning. Each day the student selects lessons from the contract, participates in group lessons, or reads silently. Daily progress is recorded on the contract.

5. The instructional program uses many books and materials. The purpose is to expand students' interests and encourage their growth through more challenging independent reading.

6. Group instruction is important. The teachers provide group instruction based on literary short stories to develop comprehension and critical thinking, using the shared inquiry approach of the Great Books program. Basic skills lessons are also provided if needed.

7. The staff works as a team. Staff configurations often include reading teachers, instructional aides, and a counselor who work together.

8. Optional features include counseling and the Preschool Story Hour. The FUTUREPRINT staff includes a full-time bilingual counselor who provides individual guidance and group counseling which focuses on improvement of communication skills, peer relationships, and academic achievement. The Preschool Story Hour gives junior high students an opportunity to read stories to preschool children from the community.

Intended Users

FUTUREPRINT is intended for all students in grades 7 and 8, but especially for students who are semi-literate or illiterate when they enter junior high. It provides a framework for individualized instruction and learning for a wide range of readers using a contract system and small-group instruction. Teachers facilitate learning as students of all reading levels become active learners.

The FUTUREPRINT Program serves an entire grade level throughout their two years at De Anza Junior High. All students enter the program as seventh graders and continue for a second year as eighth graders. The program meets the reading needs of all students, whether remedial, corrective, or developmental.

TUCSON, ARIZONA HIGH SCHOOL
MAGNET SCHOOL READING PROGRAM

Tucson High Magnet School
400 North Second Avenue
Tucson, Arizona 85705
Terry Sonnleitner, Reading Coordinator

The main focus of this program is to assist students in dealing with reading and writing activities encountered in content area classes. Some of the major goals are:

1. Create an awareness and appreciation of self.
2. Develop an ability to express thoughts and opinions orally and in writing.
3. Develop an awareness of text.
4. Develop the ability to study and manage time.
5. Increase reading comprehension skills.
6. Create an appreciation of reading for pleasure.
7. Create an awareness of events occurring at the local, state, national and world level.
8. Develop the ability to write for a variety of purposes.

Since this school is a magnet school, students who are planning to attend are tested and recommended for the program in the spring of eighth grade. The *Iowa Test of Basic Skills*, the *Nelson Test*, and a writing sample, along with teacher recommendations, are factors for entry. Criteria are the fourth stanine for standardized tests and a deficiency level on the writing sample. Students are also tested each semester to ensure proper exit from the program. There are 15 sections taught, with a maximum individual class load of 25 students.

The year begins with strategies to help students adjust to school and the changes high school brings. As the year progresses, teachers use a topical, unit approach to develop the strategies they wish students to achieve, such as biographies, oral histories, teen issues (teen pregnancy, drugs, food disorders, stress), and current events. Speakers, films, and discussion groups are also utilized as part of the program, as well as novels and journals.

Students are placed in materials suited for their reading abilities, and instruction is individualized as much as possible. Some of the materials used: *Current Science Magazine*, *Current Events Magazine*, *Cloze Connections*, *Superstars*, daily newspapers, books and tapes on how to read social studies and science and crossword puzzles. Many of the materials used are teacher-generated.

Classes in this program are taught by reading teachers (all of whom are certified to teach in other areas). However, an additional component of the program is tutorial, with time contributed by college students enrolled in teacher education classes. In one semester, 35 of these students contributed three hours a week for a total of 1,050 hours, in tutoring as well as observing teachers in the classroom. Tutoring was offered both during classes and after school, and students could receive help based on self-referral, referral by teacher, parent, counselor or administrator.

Appendix Q

UNION SPRINGS, NEW YORK
IPIMS SECONDARY READING PROGRAM
(EPTW)

IPIMS
Union Springs Central School
27 N. Cayuga Street
Union Springs, N.Y. 13160
Georgia A. Crissy, NDN Trainer-IPIMS Project
(315) 252-9309

IPIMS, or *The Individualized Prescriptive Instructional Management System for Under-achievers in Reading,* is a centrally located reading center for grades 7–12. The center is staffed by reading teachers, paraprofessionals, and student volunteers.

Essential to the center's operation is the color coding by ability level of all instructional materials. All resources are labeled and placed on the appropriate color shelf:

Yellow — grades 1–3
Blue — grades 4–6
Green — grades 7–9
Red — grades 10–12

Student folders, logs, and prescription sheets are also coded making it easier for students and staff to locate appropriate materials. Student progress is assessed by a criterion-referenced monitoring system, and reports are provided regularly to parents, teachers, and the students themselves. This approach makes best use of the human and financial resources available.

The IPIMS cycle of activities is as follows:

A. Screening and Identification of the Target Group

All students in grades 7–12 with marked deficiencies in reading are eligible for the program. Student records and the recommendations of the teaching staff determine placement within the program.

B. Diagnosis of Individual Reading Strengths and Weaknesses

In May of each academic year, students in the program are given a diagnostic reading test. These tests determine a student's placement in the Junior-Senior High School Reading Center.

167

C. Design of Individual Plan to Correct Reading Problems and Improve Skills

Test analysis determines specific correctional treatment, and individual programs are developed based on behavioral objectives.

Corrective strategies using appropriate materials are worked out cooperatively by teachers, parents, and students. Yearly goals are established. Assistance with content area courses is provided.

D. Regular Testing and Reporting of Student Progress

Student achievement is regularly tested and reported. Reading objectives are identified every six weeks and the student's mastery of these skills assessed. By clearly demonstrating their progress, students are motivated, given self-confidence and directed toward work in areas of further need.

Parents receive reports to encourage their support of the student, and the individual's progress is discussed in periodic meetings of parents, students and reading staff.

The reporting system permits modification of the student's program to meet changing needs.

E. Atmosphere and Motivation

Students receive much positive feedback in this program.

A leisure reading corner stocked with books and magazines is widely used.

Reading Center students are taken on field trips and provided with other motivating rewards.

Appendix R

URBANA, ILLINOIS
HIGH SCHOOL READING PROGRAM

Urbana High School
1002 S. Race Street
Urbana, Illinois 61801
Michael Ludwinski, Reading Supervisor
(815) 384-3682

The Reading/Writing Laboratory of Urbana High School consists of a core of eight courses which range in difficulty from late third grade to senior high level and beyond:

1	2	3	4
Basic Reading Skills	Remedial Reading I	Remedial Reading II	Developmental Reading

5	6	7	8
Humanities I	Humanities I Novel	Humanities II	Humanities II

It does not offer a clinical program or individualized one-to-one instruction; instruction is offered, instead, to small groups whose reading levels and needs are similar. The general approach to instruction is a modified version of the directed reading lesson: diagnosis and placement of students in accord with instructional levels in reading; preparation in vocabulary and essential background information; guided silent reading; oral review of what has been read; discussion of the applicability of what one has read to one's life; and testing for mastery of key skills.

The reading program addresses students' needs at both ends of the spectrum: at the lowest end are students who encounter difficulty with decoding tasks—at the other end are students who do not have decoding problems but may have poor vocabularies, deficiencies in world knowledge, and superficial reading skills. The program challenges all students to become reflective readers who are capable of valuing ideas. Many students spend only a semester in the high school reading laboratory. While there, they are taught to vary their reading approach in accordance with the purpose for which they are reading a given selection. Instruction in reading longer works, using study aids, and vocabulary is provided. Also taught is the analysis of the four major forms of discourse: description, exposition, narration, and argument.

Instead of using kits and reading skills booklets, students are given the finest literature and best written non-fiction materials suitable for their age, interests and needs. Reading instruction is organized to emphasize the humanities. Key western values are taught as a framework for presenting critical thinking skills. The "great books" approach is used, and film, art, and music are employed to promote understanding and appreciation of literature. In the Reading/Writing Lab, writing is used to clarify what has been read. The Madeline Hunter direct instruction model is used:

1. Anticipatory Set
2. Objective(s) and Purpose
3. Instructional Input
4. Modeling
5. Checking for Understanding
6. Guided Practice
7. Independent Practice

Students who have proficiency in the reading lab requirements may elect any Humanities course they have not taken. All other students are placed in the program by the high school staff after being tested regarding their proficiency. A student's reading ability is the determining factor in placement. In addition to the above courses, two other courses, COLLEGE ENTRANCE EXAMINATIONS and COLLEGE READING: THE NOVEL AND BIOGRAPHY, may be taken as electives.

VIRGINIA BEACH, VIRGINIA
JR. HIGH READING RESOURCE PROGRAM

Virginia Beach Reading Resource Program
Virginia Beach City Public Schools
P.O. Box 6038
Virginia Beach, Virginia 23456-0038
Alma Hall, Curriculum Specialist

The target population for reading instruction in the Virginia Beach Reading Resource Program is eighth grade students who are reading three or more years below their current grade placement. The program reaches many ninth grade students, also, as time and personnel are able to accommodate them. Reading resource teachers in the junior high schools examine the standardized test scores of all entering students as well as receive recommendations from classroom teachers, to determine who will enter the program.

The reading resource teacher and a full-time aide meet daily with students, usually working within the students' assigned English classroom or in some instances meeting separately with small groups of from eight to twelve students. Together, the English teacher and resource teacher plan literature units and daily activities that will reinforce the reading requirements of the English curriculum at the eighth grade level. Students are grouped within the larger class setting according to the reading and communication skills needed for a given activity. Groupings change as needs and activities change, and they receive large amounts of direct attention and opportunities for interaction with the classroom teacher, reading resource teacher, and aide.

Groupings are often made to bring together students of varying skill proficiency. One student serves as group leader and others as recorder, encourager, praiser, etc., so that each of the four to five members of the group plays a specific role. The group works on a four-to-five-day activity that is structured to elicit the contribution of each member. Some of the strategies used to meet individual student needs:

- Students choose their own novels and read each day.
- Students keep journals and share their reading responses with both teachers and peers.
- Videos on study skills offer content reading approaches beyond the English classroom.
- Film festivals provide visual lead-ins to reading selections.

- Computers and newspapers replicate real-life reading and problem-solving tasks.
- Writing helps to clarify the concepts and to explore the ideas encountered in reading.
- A balance between independent and group activities allows frequent dialogue between teachers/aides and students.
- Supplementary materials are tailored to support individual English assignments when students are experiencing difficulty.

Collaborative planning and cooperative learning are based on group dynamics and individual needs. The components come together to support teachers with materials, personnel, and reading strategies that help students to succeed.

Contributors: Mary Cade, Paula Linscott, Cele Schade, Connie Skocyznski, Jan Stark and Nancy Ward.

Appendix T

WEST ST. PAUL, MINNESOTA
RECARE HIGH SCHOOL
READING AND STUDY SKILL PROJECT (IPTW)

ReCaRe
Henry Sibley High School
1897 Delaware Avenue
West St. Paul, Minnesota 55118
Patricia S. Olson, Project Director
(612) 681-2376

ReCaRe is a high school reading and study skill project that provides:

- A management system for an individualized, heterogeneously grouped secondary reading course emphasizing four skill areas—vocabulary, reading comprehension, reading rate, and study skills.
- Immediately available short-term tutorial help for students experiencing difficulty in content-area classes.
- Teacher in-service so that reading and study skill instruction can be integrated into and reinforced in content-area classes.

In the ReCaRe course, all ability readers work side-by-side on an individualized curriculum tailored to fit their abilities, needs and interests. In addition, content-area teachers are trained to teach and reinforce the study skills emphasized in the one-semester ReCaRe course. The main objective of the program is to help all students become efficient, independent learners prior to leaving the secondary school.

THREE COMPONENTS OF THE ReCaRe PROGRAM:

COMPONENT 1

The ReCaRe Course is a semester elective for juniors and seniors. Students receive instruction 55 minutes a day for 18 weeks. The program is individualized and the curriculum takes into account pretest scores, statement of need, interest, and post high school plans. Students rotate through four skill areas: Vocabulary, Reading Rate, Study Skills, and Reading Comprehension. One day a week is set aside for group instruction to cover a variety of topics applicable to the whole class. The basic instructional sequence:

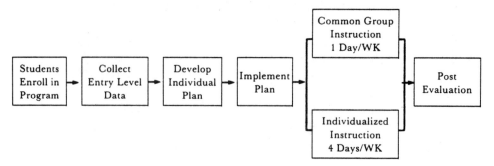

Instructional Sequence for ReCaRe Course

Each student is given a copy of the *Student Manual for the Reading Center,* a spiral-bound book, which includes class procedures and policies, a description of and directions for each of the four skill areas, the grading system, the rotation system, a statement of need, a sample Weekly Reporting Sheet, pages for each student's curriculum, and progress charts. Students in ReCaRe quickly adjust to the idea of working the entire class period and to the rigorous accountability system.

COMPONENT 2

The Referral Component operates either during the class from which the student is referred or during a student's study hall. Referral students, a maximum of 5 per hour, spend from five to ten days in the ReCaRe Center. Based on the results of informal assessment and the materials the classroom teacher plans to cover while the student is in ReCaRe, the ReCaRe teacher structures a tutorial plan. It has been found that most referred students can read and understand their course text but are seriously lacking in study skills; hence, they are inefficient readers. Study skills, such as SQ3R, note taking, and text preparation, can be practiced in a five- to ten-day period and can greatly reduce student frustration.

On the first day of a referral, the student completes an informal inventory for the text used in his/her content class, a textbook analysis sheet, which assesses understanding of the text's format, and a student information sheet, which provides insight into a student's study habits. Based on these, the ReCaRe teacher structures a tutorial plan.

COMPONENT 3

ReCaRe's Increased Teacher Awareness Component is designed to help secondary teachers integrate reading and study skill instruction into their content objectives. Since improving student learning efficiency should be a general goal of all secondary teachers, in-service training in a developmental reading program is imperative. The ReCaRe program encourages in-service sessions to acquaint secondary teachers with their role in teaching reading and study skills.

Several options are available for in-service in a teaching district:

1. The ReCaRe trainer can conduct a three-hour in-service with the whole staff. Training materials include a paper, "Reading in the Content Areas: A Search of the Literature and Annotated Bibliography of Teacher Resources."

2. An adopting district can use local reading and study skill personnel to provide in-service training.

Some provision for an all-staff workshop must be included in a ReCaRe adoption and implementation plan. Whether Component 1, 2, or 3 is selected, if teachers implement the ideas and skills presented in the in-service, ultimately all students will be more efficient, more independent learners.

SUMMARY

There are numerous conditions that must be established before an exemplary secondary reading program can be constructed. These include the development of appropriate skills and objectives, building relationships among the four language arts, and extending reading activities from the elementary school to formulate a comprehensive K–12 reading program. If a program is to be successful, trained reading specialists must be available, a sufficient budget must be provided, goals established to meet student needs, and a continuous program of evaluation provided.

The exemplary programs described in this chapter are among the best in the United States. They have been created to meet the unique needs of the students for whom they are intended. Further information can be obtained by contacting the director listed for each program.

REFERENCES

1. Early, Margaret, *Reading to Learn in Grades 5 to 12.* New York, Harcourt Brace Jovanovich, 1984, p. 106.
2. Shepherd, David L. *Comprehensive High School Reading Methods* (Second Edition). Columbus, Charles E. Merrill, 1978, p. 362.
3. Professional Standards and Ethics Committee, International Reading Association. *Guidelines for the Specialized Preparation of Reading Specialists.* Newark, Delaware, International Reading Association, 1986, p. 6 (reprinted by permission).
4. Wood, Phyllis Anderson, "Judging the Value of a Reading Program." *Journal of Reading,* Vol. 19, No. 8 (May, 1976), pp. 618–620.
5. Criscuolo, Nicholas P., "Ten Essentials for Reading Programs." *The Executive Educator,* Vol. 8, No. 3 (March, 1986), p. 18.

AUTHOR INDEX

A

Alexander, J. Estill, 127
Alkin, Marvin C., 109
Askov, Eunice N., 109

B

Balajthy, Ernest, 124, 127
Barr, Rebecca, 87
Bates, Gary W., 22, 35
Beach, Lori, 158
Becker, Brian, L. A., 66, 87
Berliner, David, 67, 87
Bettelheim, Bruno, 29, 35
Black, Dolores J., 152
Blair, Timothy R., 18, 44, 60
Bond, Guy L., 33, 35, 36
Brady, Philip, 127
Brown, Rexel, 35
Bryg, Virginia, 162
Burgess, Carol, 156
Burmeister, Lou E., 35, 110, 112, 127
Burns, Paul C., 36, 60, 88, 127

C

Cade, Mary, 172
Callaway, Byron, 35
Ciana, Alfred, 142
Clary, Lind M., 87
Claunch, Beverly, 118, 127
Coody, Betty, 18
Costa, Roberta A., 146
Criscuolo, Nicholas, 133, 175
Crissy, Georgia A., 167
Cushenbery, Donald C., 92, 109, 127

D

Dechant, Emerald V., 35, 109
Dennis, Lynn, 144

Donant, Lisbeth, 109
Dykstra, Robert, 29, 35

E

Eanet, Marilyn, 105, 110
Early, Margaret, 18, 33, 36, 60, 87, 88, 98, 109, 127, 175

F

Fernald, Grace, 31
Flood, James, 18
Forgan, Harry W., 87
Foster, Ellen D., 137, 138
Frostig, Marianne, 25
Fry, Edward, 65, 87

G

Glaser, Ann, 163
Gove, Mary K., 18
Gwaltney, Wayne, 35

H

Haddad, Heskel M., 31, 36
Hall, Alma, 171
Hardman, Patricia K., 31, 35
Harris, Albert J., 34, 87
Harris, Larry A., 109
Harris, Theodore, 31, 35
Havens, Lynn, 154
Heilman, Arthur W., 18, 44, 60
Hill, Walter R., 74, 88
Hinshelwood, James, 31
Hodges, Richard, 31, 35
Howards, Melvin, 34

I

Irwin, Patricia, 148

177

SUBJECT INDEX